# Philosophical Law

# Philosophical Law:

## AUTHORITY
## EQUALITY
## ADJUDICATION
## PRIVACY

edited by Richard Bronaugh

*Contributions in Legal Studies, Number 2*

GREENWOOD PRESS

WESTPORT, CONNECTICUT • LONDON, ENGLAND

Library of Congress Cataloging in Publication Data
Main entry under title:

Philosophical law.

   (Contributions in legal studies; no. 2 ISSN 0147-1074)
   Includes index.
   1. Sociological jurisprudence—Addresses, essays,
lectures. 2. Law—Psychology—Addresses, essays,
lectures. I. Bronaugh, Richard. II. Series.
K380.P5    340.1    77-18106
ISBN 0-8371-9809-7

Library of Congress Catalog Card Number: 77-18106
ISBN: 0-8371-9809-7
ISSN: 0147-1074

First published in 1978

Greenwood Press, Inc.
51 Riverside Avenue, Westport, Connecticut 06880

Printed in the United States of America

The quotation on page 96 is reprinted from *An Introduction to
Medieval Europe, 300-1500*, by James Westfall Thompson and
Edgar Nathaniel Johnson, by permission of W. W. Norton &
Company, Inc. Copyright 1937 by W. W. Norton & Company, Inc.
Copyright renewed 1965 by Edgar Nathaniel Johnson.

10  9  8  7  6  5  4  3  2  1

To my father

# Contents

     MARTIN P. GOLDING

10   Comment: "On the Adversary System and Justice"  122
     ROBERT S. SUMMERS

11   The Adversary System                           127
     MORLEY R. GORSKY


Part IV   PRIVACY                                   139

12   Introduction                                   141
     DAVID FLAHERTY

13   Privacy: Some Arguments and Assumptions        148
     RICHARD A. WASSERSTROM

14   Privacy, Property, Freedom, and the Family     167
     LORENNE M. G. CLARK

15   Children and Privacy                           188
     HOWARD COHEN

     Index                                          205

     About the Authors                              209

# Foreword

Human relationships can be given five distinct descriptions, four of which bear upon the topics authority, equality, adjudication, and privacy. Broadly these descriptions exhaust all the social possibilities; clearly they do so with respect to those human relations that attract the law. To see the point, imagine a pair of tin soldiers representing people in twos. First, a soldier could outrank another and be said to have authority. One soldier is "over" the other, and the two move on separate planes; this describes one type of relative standing. Many questions may be asked about this relationship. Is it just? Is it good? Is it legally valid in this instance? How was it gained? How is it held? And what exactly is the relation itself in which they stand?

A second relationship is equality. The soldiers are on a plane, upon parallel vectors in their lives. This might mean nothing more than that sergeants are or should be treated equally with sergeants and privates equally with privates. Such equality is not hostile to extensive relations of authority. Yet equality may represent a political ideal that is rather antimilitary or at least socially leveling. The difference is significant. In a third way, these soldiers may be placed in a position of combat as warriors of opposing forces. Even being at cross-purposes, being adversaries, is a type of social relationship; people often find themselves upon clashing vectors. Here the law takes an interest in the practical resolution of conflict, as it does in the philosophical nature of authority and equality. So people at odds in a legal system find their way to adjudication; the only residual form of combat permitted there is regulated within the adversary system itself.

A fourth relationship is a way of standing apart. Call it privacy. Not the mere absence of a relation, it is something that can be described as social immunization from others. Someone who enters a private zone is not just paying an unexpected visit; without explicit permission, it is an invasion. Soldiers, like children, may have little privacy—immunity may exist only in the smallest corner of their lives. The final social relationship can be described as unity. The tin soldiers are in lockstep, marching together. Congruent in their common purpose, they are free of both conflict and isolation.

Socially speaking, persons may be over others, parallel to one another, at odds, immune and isolated, or in community. From this general perspective, there seems to be·no more. The first four of these—authority, equality, adversity, and privacy—are embedded in the legal topics of the four parts of this book.

# Acknowledgments

The essays in this volume, with one exception, are previously unpublished. The collection originated with the Ninth Annual Fall Philosophy Colloquium at the University of Western Ontario in 1974. Most of the papers, and all of the lead ones, have been revised to various degrees. That colloquium was cosponsored by the Faculty of Law at Western Ontario with funds from the Josephine Spencer Niblett Foundation; Professor Iain Ramsay from that faculty shared in the work of the conference. The Canada Council, as it so often has, gave us financial assistance as well. The editor expresses his gratitude.

I should like to thank Professor David Flaherty of the Department of History at the University of Western Ontario for his introduction to the section on privacy. Professor Flaherty is co-principal investigator of the Ford Foundation Project on Privacy and Access to Government Data for Social Science Research. I should also like to thank Alice, my wife, for proofreading and Pat Orphan for typing and careful attention to the manuscript.

# Part I. AUTHORITY

# Introduction

## RICHARD BRONAUGH

I am robbed; I am taxed. By their fruits I shall not know the difference for they are impositions that make me equally poor. One well-
known philosopher of law has said that a distinction at least can be
marked by noticing that I am obliged by the robber and obligated to
the taxman. Does this mean that when I am obliged I am forced, and
when obligated I am not? Well, in a manner of speaking, both
parties wield guns and say to me, "Your money or your life!" Compare the pickpocket. He gives me no opportunity to lay down my life
for my purse. He leaves me no choice at all. Unlike the pickpocket,
the taxman and the robber, equally in this regard, get their ways by
threat-advantage. They change the likely payoffs and render some
acts of mine less eligible than they otherwise would have seemed
while making others almost appear necessary—though not really.
Neither taxman nor robber does what the pickpocket does; neither
deprives me of both my purse and my freedom of choice in a deft
motion. What I do not like about the taxman and the robber is their
manipulation of the natural consequences of the choices with which
I am left. But bad choices are still choices. Now a logician has
shown how obligation to the taxman might be reduced to something
quite familiar and truth functional: "Necessarily, if you don't do $X$,
then a Bad Thing happens." But it's the same game. Perhaps there
is some point to thinking it over after all—as I pay.

Taxation, I am told, is not theft because it is a function of legitimate political authority; the office is downtown. Robbers, on the
other hand, often have no fixed addresses. The robber who acts
"with authority" does so without the color of right, however so
forcible and agile he may be. Of course, to have the color of right is
not to be right, so one might be an illegitimate authority. But the

first question, about the general nature and concept of authority, is what one claims to *have* in one's possession of it, or what it is someone thinks another has in one's submission to authority. What is *purported?* Merely to ask how the strong are to justify themselves (though a proper question of morality) does not yet raise a question of authority. Just as alienation from brute power evidences nothing more than weakness, so secured power shows strength but gives no understanding of authority itself. One must ask what the taxman has, even when he is ineffective, and what the robber lacks, even though he is strong over many a dark night. Compare the fraudulent person. She is a robber trying to look good, and she may often try to wear a mask of authorization. At least, she claims to *have authority,* however spurious her claim may be. What is it that the taxman and the fraudulent person have in common that distinguishes them from the holdup man and the pickpocket? Clearly the first two purport to have authority.

Joseph Raz, in the following paper, attempts to state an analysis of the concept of authority, which is disengaged from several questions: how one might have come to be in the position of an authority, how a justification is provided for someone's effective authority, how one gets and holds de facto power by force, and when it is that rules confer authority in social contexts. His task is to give a proper "explanation of what it is to have authority" as such without settling questions of acquisition, legitimacy, or conferment.

Assume that I have authority to examine your tax returns. Having the authority to perform certain actions respecting your returns is not the same as being an authority over your person. As a tax examiner I cannot alter your normative position in the world, which is what an authority can do. There is someone who has that position, which comes to him through his possession of normative power. An authority who has normative power (for example, the minister of revenue) has authority over me and over you. His normative power consists in being able to empower me, as a tax examiner, to do something that, when it affects your interests, is said to be an authorized action. On doing this, the authority actually has altered the normative position of us both and has given me authority to act with respect to you in a certain way. In that fashion I have authority to examine your returns. Obviously the robber who rifles your files while holding you at gunpoint is in no such position. His normative position was not altered by an authority. He has not been permitted to do this to you; he has no authority, though he does possess, like an official, a certain threat-advantage. He may succeed in altering your financial picture, but he does not have authority to alter your reasons for action.

Raz's analysis also provides an explanation of normative power. This possibility of normative power, or at least the species *authority,* has seemed to some philosophers to be a danger to man's rational and moral autonomy. That is, to be responsive to command is to go blind; it is to surrender the determination of one's action "upon the balance of the reasons of which one is aware." If this state of affairs were true, then no authority would be justifiable or legitimate since submission would be immoral and irrational. This is quite naturally thought to be a paradoxical outcome; being an authority would seem something like having purchase on souls. The difficulty can be resolved, according to Raz, by combining his analysis of what it is to have authority with his analysis of the relation between normative power and reasons for action. Normative power is the ability to change certain of those reasons; it is doing what alters someone's normative position. Thus if an authority $X$, a type of normative powerholder, issues an order to $Y$ *to* $\phi$ (to do some action, such as audit $Z$'s returns), then $Y$ has a new reason to $\phi$ and his normative position is altered. Not only does he have a new (pro) reason but also, in the same stroke according to Raz, he has an "exclusionary reason," which is a reason to eschew certain (con) reasons. A reason with this sort of duality is called a "protected reason" and can be established only through the exercise of an authority's normative power. The paradoxes of authority arise because action upon the balance of the reasons of which one is aware is mistakenly thought to be the only form of moral rationality. But to act upon protected reasons and to recognize their exclusionary aspect is also rational; thus obedience to authority is not a betrayal of one's autonomy. At least that is the conclusion reached by Dr. Raz.

# On legitimate authority

**JOSEPH RAZ**

### The Paradoxes

There is little surprise that the notion of authority is one of the most controversial concepts found in the armory of legal and political philosophy. Its central role in any discussion of legitimate forms of social organization and of legitimate forms of political action makes the indefinite continuation of this controversy inevitable. The immediate relevance of the problem of authority to current controversial issues makes a dispassionate study of the subject all the more difficult. But beyond these extrinsic difficulties, the study of the concept of authority has to confront two major problems of intellectual origin: the methodological problem of how to avoid confusing the various quite distinct problems involving the notion of authority and the paradoxes of authority.

The paradoxes of authority can assume different forms, but all of them concern the alleged incompatibility of authority with reason or autonomy. To be subjected to authority, it is argued, is incompatible with reason, for reason requires that one should always act on the balance of reasons of which one is aware.[1] It is of the nature of authority that it requires submission even when one thinks that what is required is against reason. Therefore, submission to authority is irrational. Similarly the principle of autonomy entails action on one's own judgment on all moral questions. Since authority sometimes requires action against one's own judgment, it requires abandoning one's moral autonomy. Since all practical questions may involve moral considerations, all practical authority denies moral autonomy and is consequently immoral.[2]

Arguments along these lines do not challenge the coherence of the notion of authority nor do they deny that some people are believed to have authority or actually have de facto authority. They challenge the possibility of legitimate, justified, *de jure* authority. Their paradoxical nature derives not from their denial of legitimate authority but from the fact that the denial is alleged to derive from the very nature of morality or from fundamental principles of rationality. Moreover the arguments challenge the legitimacy not only of political authority but of all authority over rational persons.[3] If the very nature of authority is incompatible with the idea of morality and rationality, then those who believe in legitimate authority are not merely wrong or mistaken in one of their moral beliefs. They are committed to an irrational belief or are guilty of a fundamental misapprehension of the concept of morality or of authority. This gives these arguments a much greater force. They are, for example, immune from most skeptical arguments. For even if there is no way of distinguishing between right and wrong substantive moral beliefs, at least we can clarify moral concepts and establish relations of entailment and incompatibility between them. If the very concepts of morality and rationality are incompatible with that of authority, then even the skeptic will be able to know that all authority is immoral and submission to it is irrational.

Paradoxically the very force of these arguments is their weakness. Many who will be willing to accept lesser challenges to legitimate authority will be reluctant to accept this most powerful challenge. Many who will be ready to accept that many authorities are not legitimate, even that no political authority is ever legitimate, will be deterred by the thought that no authority can ever be legitimate. Many who will be ready to concede that those who believe in the possibility of legitimate authority are wrong will shy away from the thought that they are irrational or have no idea what morality is about.

It is not my aim to examine the ways in which authority can be defended or attacked. But since the arguments, on which the paradoxes are based, are said to derive all their force from the analysis of the concepts of authority, morality, and rationality, their examination is relevant to any attempt to clarify the notion of authority. I am concerned here with the nature of authority. I shall try to show why the concept of authority gives rise to the apparent paradoxes and why they are merely apparent. I am not the first to try to dissolve the paradoxes, and it is not part of my brief that all previous attempts to do so failed. I think, however, that the analysis that follows, even if proving a known truth, does so in a novel way, which shows both the temptation and the fallacies of the paradoxes to best advantage.

## A Methodological Detour

Some of the classical authors sought to explain the nature of authority by explaining the way in which people come to accept the authority of individuals or groups. Discussions of the concept were mixed with descriptions of the evolution of society, of conquests, or of social contracts. Modern authors have avoided this confusion, but discussion of the subject is still bedeviled with many methodological confusions. I shall describe briefly four of the common types of explanation and try to point to the lessons to be learned from their shortcomings.

1. The first standard explanation consists in specifying the conditions that are in fact either necessary or sufficient for holding an effective (a de facto) authority. But such explanations fail to elucidate the nature of authority in any way at all. To be sure, it is an important part of social theory to explain under what conditions people can obtain or hold authority, under what circumstances a community is likely to accept the authority of some persons. But they fail altogether to explain what these conditions are for, what it is to have authority or to be in authority.

2. The second type of explanation attempts to elucidate the nature of authority by describing the necessary or sufficient conditions for the holding of a legitimate (*de jure*) authority.

This second pattern of explanation seems more promising. According to it the concept of authority is to be explained by explaining how claims of authority can be justified. The force of such explanations is clear. They do not presuppose that claims of authority can in fact ever be justified, but merely point out how they are to be justified. On the reasonable assumption that claims of authority are a way of justifying action, it seems almost inevitable that they differ from other justifications of action by the type of justificative arguments involved. In fact this conclusion is far from inevitable. Justifying claims may differ not only in the nature of the justifying argument invoked but also in the nature of the act justified.

There is a considerable initial plausibility in the idea that authority is to be explained by reference to the kind of act, for example, a claiming, it justifies. We certainly need authority to perform some actions but not others, and it appears at least prima facie that to say that one has a certain authority is to indicate that one could be either justified or capable of doing certain actions, without committing oneself in any way as to the nature of that justification.

Here lies the major problem of justificative analyses of authority. None has so far succeeded in delineating the type of argument that amounts to a claim of authority. The fact that there are many different types of authority concerned with virtually every sphere of human activity makes one inclined to give up hope that such a delineation is possible. We can exemplify this difficulty by considering an interesting attempt made recently to provide a justificative analysis of authority. Richard Tuck has suggested that citations of political authority are statements designed to kill criticism of a political action but are not authentic justifications.[4] They are based on the claim that the action is right if one person performs it, though it is neither right nor wrong that the person who claims authority should be that one person, and that person is actually performing the action for which the authority is claimed.

Many will share Tuck's belief that nobody has a right to a position of (political) authority and that the only way to justify political authority is by the use of arguments of the type he outlined. But we all know that some thought that some people are by nature slaves and that those who are by nature free have authority over them. Others believed in the divine right of kings, and there are and were other theories asserting that some people have a right and a duty by nature or by reason to rule. Such people, let us assume, are wrong. But are they also guilty of misusing language, as Tuck's approach suggests? Is the mistake one of moral and political theory, or is it also a mistake about the meaning of words, about the concept of authority?

All other justificative explanations have to overcome the same difficulty. It is not enough to establish that only arguments of a certain type can justify authority. One has to show that claiming authority on any other grounds is a misuse of language.

The criticism of the first two patterns of explanation points to a clear lesson: the analysis of authority cannot consist exclusively of an elucidation of the conditions under which one has either legitimate or effective authority. It must explain what one has when one has authority. This strongly suggests that authority is an ability to perform certain kinds of action.[5] The analysis I proposed here is meant to vindicate this suggestion.

3. One popular theory that regards authority as ability to perform certain kinds of action identifies effective (de facto) authority with power over people. I shall suggest later that to have authority over persons is to have normative power. But it is a different notion of power that is involved here. According to it to have power is to have influence, to be able to influence people's actions and their fortunes. A person has effective authority if he is powerful, if he can influence people's fate and their choices or options.[6] Legitimate authority can then be defined as justified effective authority.[7] It is effective authority that should be preserved or obeyed (subject to various conditions and qualifications).

For several reasons, however, it seems that such theories put the cart before the horse. The notion of legitimate authority is in fact the primary one. For one thing not all legitimate authority is effective. Besides (as I will claim shortly), the notion of effective authority cannot be explained except by reference to legitimate authority. Several considerations should be borne in mind.

• Though our concern is with practical rather than theoretical authority, an analysis maximizing the similarities between authority for action and authority for belief is—other things being equal—preferable. It seems clear that scientific genius can go unrecognized and that a man who is in fact the greatest authority in a certain field may have very little influence over people's research or their beliefs on issues within his competence.

• Parents have authority over their children regardless of whether their children actually acknowledge their authority. Admittedly parental authority is usually recognized by other adults, but that is the wrong sort of recognition from the point of view of a recognition theory, which holds that it is recognition by the subjects that matters. Parental authority does not depend on recognition.

• If theoretical authority does not entail recognition or enforcement, then there must be at least some cases of practical authority that also do not entail recognition or enforcement. There are practical authorities whose authority is based entirely on their being theoretical authorities: an expert doctor is an authority not only on the causes of illness but also on their cures. There are experts on the stock exchange and experts on navigation and many others who are authorities for action in their field even though their authority may be unrecognized and unenforced.

• I share the belief that a legitimate political authority is of necessity effective at least to a degree. But this is a result of substantive political principles (such as that one of the main justifications for having a political authority is its usefulness in securing social coordination, and that knowledge and expertise do not give one a right to govern and play only a subordinate role in the justification of political authority). It is not entailed by a conceptual analysis of the notion of authority, not even by that of the concept of political authority.

The analysis of legitimate authority is not by itself sufficient to explain our notion of authority. A complete account must include an analysis of effective authority as well. Having argued that the notion of legitimate authority does not presuppose that of effective authority,[8] it may be worth pointing out that the reverse is not true. The notion of legitimate authority is presupposed by that of effective authority. A person needs more than power (as influence) to have de facto authority. He must either claim that he has legitimate authority or be held by others to have legitimate authority. There is an important difference, for example, between the brute use of force to get one's way and the same done with a claim of right. Only the latter can qualify as an effective or de facto authority. But this is a problem that cannot be explored here.

4. Some people hold that authority must be defined by reference to rules: that a person has authority means that there is a system of rules, which confers authority on him. This mode of explanation is in fact a variant of the first and second patterns of explanation and is open to the same basic objection. It substitutes a claim as to

when people have authority for a proper explanation of what it is to have authority. It states that people have authority only when it is conferred on them by some rules. But it does not provide any means of deciding which rules confer authority and which do not. Some rules will, it is true, confer authority quite explicitly. They have authoritative, binding formulations (enacted rules), and their authoritative formulations specify that they confer authority on a certain person. But the proposed definition does nothing to illuminate their meaning and effect.

The claim that all authority is conferred by rules is itself debatable. It seems difficult to maintain that when a member of the public assumes authority in an emergency (for example, a fire in a theatre) his authority derives from any rules. It is not, however, my purpose here to discuss the ways authority can be acquired or defended. There are other objections to definitions of this type. Unless properly qualified they entail contradictions. If there are two systems of rules according to one of which a certain person has authority whereas according to the other he does not, then he both has and does not have authority. To avoid such contradiction the proposed definition must be relativized. It cannot be taken to be a definition of having authority but of the relativized notion of having authority according to $s$ where $s$ is some system of rules. The relativized notion of authority, however, severs the connection between authority and practical reason.

Authority is a practical concept. This means that questions of who has authority over whom are practical questions; they bear on what one ought to do. In other words statements that some persons have authority may serve as premises in practical inferences. The explanation of authority must explain the practical import of the concept. It must explain how it is capable of figuring in practical inferences.

What one ought to do depends on who has authority in a nonrelativized sense. That a person has authority according to some system of rules is, in itself, of no practical relevance. Just as one can draw no conclusions as to what ought to be done from the fact that according to a certain person authority is vested in Parliament, so one cannot draw any such conclusions from the fact that according to some rules, authority is vested in Parliament. Certain further assumptions may entail that if according to someone Parliament has authority, then Parliament does have authority. Similarly further assumptions may allow a move from a statement of authority according to some rules to a nonrelativized statement of authority. It would be a mistake, however, to build those further conditions into one's definition of "authority according to some rules" so as to make the move to a nonrelativized statement of authority always possible. The whole purpose of talk of relativized authority is to block the possibility of such a move, unless further assumptions are available. We need such a device to be able to talk of the views of other people about authority, of the situation according to rules accepted in some societies or proposed by some people. To do this we have in talk of relativized authority a way to refer to what those people or societies accept or propose as legitimate authority without endorsing those views. We simply state what authority is had by whom from a certain point of view.[9] In some circumstances the fact that some people hold certain views or endorse certain rules is enough to invest a person with authority. In others it is not. The move from a relativized statement of authority to a nonrelativized one is never automatic and is not always possible.

These considerations suggest that the nonrelativized notion is the primary one. The relativized notion is useful because it reveals the views of people or societies concerning nonrelativized authority. Its explanation presupposes the nonrelativized notion, which does not presuppose it. Our task then is to explain the notion of legitimate nonrelativized authority in a way that shows its relevance to practical reasoning.

### The Simple Explanation

Several authors have analyzed authority along the lines I recommended. On the whole there is a large measure of agreement between them but they differ greatly in important details. Robert Paul Wolff, to take one well-known example, says that "authority is the right to command, and correlatively, the right to be obeyed."[10] His definition is essentially sound but it is both inaccurate and not perspicuous. It is inaccurate, for authority is a right to do other things as well. It can be a right to legislate, to grant permissions, to give authoritative advice, to adjudicate, and so forth. It is wrong to regard all these as commanding. Wolff's definition is not perspicuous since the notion of a right is even more complex and problematic than that of authority.

To be useful the analysis must be made in terms of relatively simple concepts. From this point of view I think that the best existing explanation of authority is that offered by John Lucas: "A man, or body of men, *has authority* if it follows from his saying 'Let $X$ happen,' that $X$ ought to happen."[11] This definition is both perspicuous and general. It applies to all types of practical authority over persons and not merely to political authority. It makes clear that one can exercise authority not only by commanding but in other ways as well.[12] I think that Lucas's definition is basically sound, and, therefore, I can make it the starting point of my examination of the concept.

Lucas explains authority as an ability to perform an action, and he regards the relevant action as that of changing the normative situation. I shall assume that if $X$ ought to $\phi$ then he has reason to $\phi$ and that if he has reason to $\phi$ then he ought to $\phi$. On this assumption Lucas's definition entails that a person has authority if his saying, "Let $X$ happen," is a reason for $X$ to happen. This sounds somewhat incongruous. The reason is that Lucas's definition does not make clear that the authority he is defining is authority over persons. To make this assumption clear we can further amend his definition and say that $X$ has authority over $Y$ if his saying, "Let $Y$ $\phi$," is a reason for $Y$ to $\phi$. Let us call this the simple analysis.

Two comments are in place here. First, I do not claim that authority can be explained only in terms of reasons. The preference for a reason-based explanation is motivated by a belief that reasons provide the ultimate basis for the explanation of all practical concepts, namely, that all must be explained by showing their relevance to practical inferences. The preference for reason-based explanations of authority is one for trying to show the role of authority statements in practical reasoning directly rather than through the mediation of other concepts (such as rights). Second, a great variety of things are called reasons. That it rains, for example, is a reason for carrying an umbrella. So is the fact that one wants to be outside and not to get wet. But in a perfectly straightforward sense both are just parts of one reason. We can distinguish between partial reasons and the complete reasons of which they are parts. It is in terms of complete reasons that the attempt to analyze authority will be made.[13] I shall argue below that the simple explanation fails to distinguish adequately between intentional and nonintentional exercise of authority and that it does not pay attention to the distinction between being an authority and having authority. It also overlooks the fact that one needs authority to grant permissions and to confer powers. But first I shall examine some more far-reaching objections to it.

### First Objection to the Simple Explanation

Is the utterance of an authority an absolute or a prima facie reason for doing as it demands? If we assume that it is an absolute reason, then it seems very unlikely that there are any legitimate authorities, and there seem to be very few de facto authorities. I, for example, believe that I am justified in taking the advice, commands, or rules issued by some people as reasons for action, but I cannot see that it is ever right to take anybody's word as an absolute reason to be followed under all circumstances. It seems to me that this is a widely shared view and that most people hold that under certain circumstances the instructions of authority need not be followed. Hence if authority is explained in terms of ability to issue absolutely binding instructions, then there seem to be very few recognized authorities in the world and none which is legitimate.

But are authoritative utterances prima facie reasons? Compare an order with a request and both with advice. All three are identified by the attitudes, beliefs, and intentions of their source, not by the way they are received by their addressee. The fact that one was ordered or requested or advised to take a certain action may be a reason to take it, and it may be held by the addressee to be so. Under different circumstances the fact that such utterances were made is no reason for action or is not held to be one. From the addressee's point of view there is no necessary difference between being ordered, being requested, and being advised except that they entail or imply different intentions, beliefs, or attitudes in the person issuing them.

One such difference is that the primary intention in advising is to convey information about what is morally right or wrong, what is lawful or unlawful, in one's interests or not, and so forth or just about brute facts. If there is an intention to influence the addressee (and there need not be one) then it is to influence him by making him aware of the situation (for example, that he ought to $\phi$ or that $\phi$-ing will secure the greatest income possible in the circumstances).

In short the advisor must intend his giving the advice to be taken as a reason to believe that what he says is true, correct, or justified. But he does not necessarily intend it to be taken as a reason for action, even though it may be the case that his giving the advice is a valid reason for action for the recipient.

Requesting and ordering, on the other hand, entail intending that the act of requesting or ordering be taken as a reason to perform the act ordered or requested. What then is the difference between them? One such difference is relevant to our purpose. Suppose that a man makes a request and is told in reply that his request was considered, but on balance it was found that the reasons against the action requested overrode those for it including the request itself. He will no doubt be disappointed but he will not feel that his request was disregarded. He has nothing to complain about. He must concede that whatever his hopes he intended no more than that the action be taken on the balance of reasons, his request being one of them.[14] This is not so if he gave an order. A man who orders someone else does not regard his order as merely another reason to be added to the balance by which the addressee will determine what to do. He intends the addressee to take his order as a reason on which to act regardless of whatever other conflicting reasons exist (short usually of an emergency or other extreme circumstances).[15]

It may seem that the explanation of this difference is that a man issuing an order always intends it to be a very weighty reason and that is not always the case when people make requests. Apart from the fact that some requests are made with such an intention, this explanation seems unsatisfactory because it relies on an alleged difference in degree. If the difference indicated is the one crucial to the distinction between orders and requests, then it is unlikely to be one of degree only.

The crucial point of this objection is that one requires authority to be entitled to command but one does not need authority to be entitled to request. My point is not that everyone is entitled to request. Whether this is the case is a moral, not a conceptual, question. There is nothing in the concept of a request that entails that everyone is entitled to request. My point is that the fact that one is entitled to request does not entail that one has authority over the addressee of the request. Contrariwise, that one is entitled to command entails that one has authority over the addressee of the command. A request made by a person entitled to make it is a valid (prima facie) reason for its addressee. Similarly a command issued by a person entitled to issue it is valid. If we are to say no more than that a valid command is a reason for its addressee, then we fail to explain the difference between a command and a request and the reason for which only entitlement to the first entails having authority. To say that a valid command is a weightier reason than a valid request is both false and inadequate as an explanation of a distinction that is not merely one of degree.

## Second Objection to the Simple Explanation

The first objection was based on an argument to the effect that if authority is ability to change reasons by certain utterances, then the utterances of authority are more than prima facie yet less than absolute reasons, which is an impossibility. The second objection is based on an argument to the effect that the utterances of (legitimate) authority though often reasons for action need not always be so.[16] It consists of an appeal to our intuition based on a counter-example. Consider the following situation. I am driving my car in flat country with perfect visibility and there is no other human being, animal, or car for miles around me. I come to a traffic light showing red. Do I have any reason to stop? There is no danger to anyone and whatever I do will not be known to anyone and will not affect my own attitude, feelings, or beliefs about authority in the future. Many will say that there is not even the slightest reason to stop at the red light in such circumstances.[17] They insist that this in no way contradicts their acknowledgment of the legitimate authority of those who made the traffic regulations. This example seems sufficient to convince one that in this case or a similar case the utterances of authority can be held to be legitimate without holding them to constitute reasons for action.

I think that these objections are sufficient to undermine the simple explanation and yet the simple explanation is right in its basic insight—that authority is ability to change reasons for action. Both the simple explanation and the objections to it are based on an over-restricted view of reasons for action. I shall argue below that if we regard authority as ability to change a certain type of reason, then the objections can be easily answered.

### Normative Power

Consider any situation in which an authority instructs a subordinate to follow the instruction of another whose authority does not derive from that of the first. A father telling his son to obey his mother is such a case. It differs from the father telling the son to obey his nanny, since the nanny's authority derives from that of the parents. An instruction to obey the nanny is, we may assume, her only source of authority. The mother's instructions are in any case authoritative. They are reasons for action for the son. So are the father's instructions. His instruction to obey the mother is, therefore, a reason to act for a reason. It is a reason to act on the mother's instruction, which is itself a reason anyway. I shall call a reason to act for a reason a positive second-order reason. There are also negative second-order reasons, that is, reasons to refrain from acting for a reason. I shall call negative second-order reasons exclusionary reasons. To get an example of an exclusionary reason we need only reverse the father's instruction and assume that he orders his son not to act on his mother's orders.[18] Now the son has a reason for not acting on a reason.

There is one important point to bear in mind concerning second-order reasons: they are reasons for action, the actions concerned being acting for a reason and not acting for a reason. If $P$ is a reason to $\phi$ then acting for the reason that $P$ is $\phi$-ing for the reason that $P$. Not acting for $P$ is not $\phi$-ing for the reason that $P$. This is compatible with $\phi$-ing for some other reason as well as with not $\phi$-ing at all. I am not assuming that whenever one fails to act on a reason one does so intentionally. One may fail to act on a reason because one does not know of its existence. These clarifications make it plain that in the examples I am assuming that in telling his son to obey his mother, the father tells him not merely to do what she tells him to do but also to do it for the reason that she tells him so. Similarly I am assuming that when the father tells his son not to obey his mother, he is not telling him never to do what his mother tells him to do but merely never to take her instructions as reasons for action.

Sometimes a person may have a reason for performing an action and also a reason for not acting for certain reasons against that very action. The son, in our example, may know that his only coat is ugly. This is a reason against wearing it. It conflicts with his mother's instruction to wear a coat when he goes out at night. But the reason against wearing the coat is reinforced indirectly by the father's order to disregard the mother's instruction. In this and many other cases the fact that is a reason (the father's order) for disregarding certain reasons (the mother's instruction) for $\phi$-ing (wearing the coat) is different from any fact that is a reason (the coat's ugliness) for not $\phi$-ing. But sometimes the same fact is both a reason for an action and an (exclusionary) reason for disregarding reasons against it. I shall call such facts protected reasons for an action.

I will define normative power as ability to change protected reasons. More precisely, a man has normative power if he can by an action of his exercise normative power. An act is the exercise of a normative power if there is sufficient reason for regarding it either as a protected reason or as canceling protected reasons and if the reason for so regarding it is that it is desirable to enable people to change protected reasons by such acts, if they wish to do so.[19]

I shall assume that power is used by making what I shall call power-utterances. There are three ways in which the power holders can change protected reasons that are important to our purpose. The first is by issuing an exclusionary instruction, that is, by using power to tell a person to $\phi$, the power-utterance is a reason for that person to $\phi$ and also a second-order reason for not acting on (all or some) reasons for not $\phi$-ing. Exclusionary instructions are, therefore, protected reasons. The second way of exercising power is by making a power-utterance granting permission to perform an action hitherto prohibited by an exclusionary instruction. I shall call such permissions canceling permissions for they cancel exclusionary reasons. The third form of using power is by conferring power on a person. This does not in itself change protected reasons but it enables a person to change them. The power a person has can be restricted in many ways—in the way it can be exercised, the persons over whom it is held, the actions with respect of which the power holder can make power-utterances, and so forth.

Given these clarifications it is evident that there is a close relation between normative power and authority. On the simple explanation of authority power is a special case of authority. Authority is ability to change reasons. Power is ability to change a special type of reasons—protected ones. However, in light of the objections to the simple explanation, I suggest that we should regard authority basically as a species of power. To provide a comprehensive defense of this view requires showing that rules and commands are protected reasons and that all authoritative utterances are power-utterances. This is not a task that can be accomplished in this article. Instead I shall try to provide a persuasive case showing first that the two objections fail against this view and, second, that the paradoxes can be explained away by it. But before I defend my view let me first explain it.

### Power and Authority

We should distinguish between authority over persons and authority to perform certain actions. The two overlap but are distinct though related notions. Everyone who is an authority has authority over people, but not everyone who has authority is an authority. The difference is not of great philosophical moment, but its neglect can be a source of endless confusion. A person is an authority if he has relatively permanent and pervasive authority over persons, that is, either authority over a large group of people or with respect to various spheres of activity, or both.

Since power is the ability to change protected reasons for action and as reasons for action are reasons for some persons or others, we can divide powers into powers over oneself and powers over others. Perhaps the most important species of power over oneself is the power to undertake voluntary obligations. Power over others is authority over them. There is one exception to this characterization. Sometimes we say that a person has authority over himself. This is a degenerate case of authority: an extension by analogy from the central cases of authority over others. It is interesting to note that when speaking of a person's authority over himself, we always refer to his power to grant himself permissions or powers. We never refer thus to one's power to undertake voluntary obligations.

One of the main obstacles to an analysis of authority is the frequent failure to distinguish between authority to perform an action and authority over persons.[20] A person has authority to perform an action if he was given permission to perform it or was given power to perform it by somebody who has power to do so. Thus, I have authority to open your mail if the censor gave me permission to do so, assuming that he has power to do so.

My authority to open your mail is not authority over you. I cannot change your normative situation in any way though the censor changed it by giving me the authority to open your mail, thereby diminishing your right to privacy. I can also have authority to sign checks in your name, which is a power I have because you gave it to me. This last example shows that the source of a person's authority to perform an act must have power to confer it, but he need not have authority over the person on whom he confers authority. To give me authority to sign checks in your name you need power but that you have such a power does not entail that you have any authority over me. It may well be that you have none.

The authority to act is, however, closely related to authority over persons, albeit in a somewhat more indirect way. When we consider the cases in which we are granted permissions or powers it is evident that not all of them can be described as having authority to act. Only when the interests of another person will be affected by the act do we speak of it as authorized. But this is not a sufficient condition. I am permitted to.open a supermarket that will lead to someone's bankruptcy, and yet it is not the case that I have authority to open the supermarket. I am permitted to do so simply because there is not and never was a prohibition to do so. One has authority to do only those things that one is given permission to do by somebody who has authority over the person whose interests are affected.

We can now define *X has authority to* $\phi$ as: there is some *Y* and there is some *Z* such that, for *X*,

(1) *Y* permitted *X* to $\phi$ or gave him power to do so
(2) *Y* has power to do so
(3) *X*'s $\phi$-ing will affect the interests of *Z* and *Y* has authority over *Z*.[21]

## Refuting the Objections

The distinctions between being an authority and having authority and between authority to act or authority over persons are not directly connected with my claim that authority over persons, the basic of the three concepts, is a species of normative power. These distinctions must be preserved by any account of authority. The advantage of the power analysis of authority is that it successfully meets the objection to the simple explanation and dissolves the paradoxes of authority.

Take the first objection first. Authority over persons is ability to change protected reasons for their actions. In most discussions of the concept of authority attention is focused on issuing orders and laying down rules as the standard manifestations of authority. These are, indeed, the standard cases of the intentional invocation of authority. It is, however, important to see that authority can be exercised without the person having authority intending to invoke it. This is true of political as well as of other kinds of authority and is a very important channel for the influence of authority to be felt. I shall take advice given by authority as a typical case in point.

Advice, whatever the hopes of the advisor may be, is given with the intention that its utterance will be taken as a reason for belief, not for action.[22] But the recipient of the advice may regard it as both a reason for action and an exclusionary reason for disregarding conflicting reasons. Consider the standard grounds for seeking advice. These are usually to gain information relevant to the solution of some practical problem facing one or for comparing one's own evaluation of the weight and importance of various factors with that of other people as a means of checking one's own views and calculations. But sometimes advice is sought for entirely different reasons. A person may be faced with a problem involving considerations concerning which he has little knowledge or understanding. He may turn to an expert, to an authority, for advice despite the fact that he has no way of assessing the reasons pointed out by the authority against other conflicting reasons of which he may be aware. He may decide to follow the advice given without trying to work out whether it indicates reasons that tip the balance. If he does so he is in fact excluding all the conflicting reasons of which he is aware from his considerations. He is regarding the advice both as a reason to perform the action he was advised to perform and for not acting on conflicting reasons. A person may be justified in holding the advice he received to be a protected reason, even though advice is not given with an intention to be taken as a protected reason.

Orders, on the other hand, are given with the intention that their addressees shall take them as protected reasons. Many people can give an order without being entitled to do so. They are entitled to do so only if they have authority (power) over the addressee with respect to the subject matter of the order. The order may be a valid first-order reason for performing the act even if it is not a valid exclusionary reason not to act on conflicting reasons, and it may be both even though the person who issued it has no authority to do so. But it always is a valid first order and an exclusionary reason if he has the authority to give it.

Exclusionary reasons may exclude action for all or only for some kinds of the conflicting reasons. Exclusionary reasons differ in scope, that is, in the extent to which they exclude different kinds of conflicting reasons. Therefore, to maintain that orders are both first-order and exclusionary reasons is not tantamount to maintaining that they are absolute reasons. They may not exclude certain conflicting reasons, and when this is the case one must decide what to do on the balance of the nonexcluded first-order reasons, including the order itself as one prima facie reason for the performance of the ordered action.

What then is the difference between an exclusionary reason and a first-order reason of a weight sufficient to override all the conflicting reasons that are excluded by the exclusionary reason and no others? There are two answers to this crucial question. First, exclusionary reasons exclude by kind and not by weight. They may exclude all the reasons of a certain kind (such as, considerations of economic welfare), including very weighty reasons, while not excluding even trivial considerations belonging to another kind (such as, considerations of honor). Second, regardless of the different impact of exclusionary and weighty reasons on what ought to be done, all things considered, they also differ in the way we view them. Some facts are weighty reasons overriding conflicting reasons; others are not to be compared with conflicting reasons. Their impact is not to change the balance of reasons but to exclude action on the balance of reasons.

This difference in function, regardless of any possible difference in what ought to be done, all things considered, explains the difference between orders and requests. Valid orders are not necessarily more weighty or important reasons than valid requests. There could be orders that exclude few conflicting considerations and that do not exclude and may be overridden by certain requests. A request may be a reason of sufficient weight to justify sacrificing one's life. The difference is not in importance but in mode of operation. A request is made with the intention that it shall be taken as a reason for action and be acceded to only if it tips the balance. Orders are made with the intention that they should prevail in certain circumstances even if they do not tip the balance. They are intended to be taken as reasons for excluding certain others that may tip the balance against performing that action.

Put it another way. For every order, if we know what the person who issued it thinks is the correct outcome of all possible practical conflicts in which it may be involved, we can ascribe to him the view that his order has just the weight that would justify all those consequences. But in doing this we have not advanced at all toward explaining the difference between orders and requests in general. This can be done if there is a certain constant weight, or range of weights, that is characteristic of all orders and distinguishes them from requests. But in fact both orders and requests span the whole range of possible weights both in the eyes of those who issued them and of others. Having assumed that the difference between them lies in their practical implications, I submit that it consists in the fact that orders but not requests are protected reasons.

There is a minimum that an order must exclude to be an order. It must at least exclude considerations of the recipient's present desires. Often orders exclude much more besides but never do they exclude less. In appropriate circumstances one may be able to justify one's not having followed an order on the ground that the order was not intended to apply to the case. It was never intended, he could claim, that he should obey even if it turned out that there was a strong moral reason for not doing so or if obeying would severely damage the recipient's interests or be unlawful.[23] When such considerations amount to a justification and lead the agent not to follow the order, he cannot be said to have obeyed it but neither did he disobey it. It was not intended that he should follow it in such circumstances. But it is never a justification that the agent had a desire, however strong, for something inconsistent with his following the order. Many parents' orders come near to the minimum exclusion, being intended to exclude only consideration of the child's present desires in order to avoid argument on what is best given his strong desire to perform or to avoid some action. But parents' orders often exclude a consideration of the child's own interests and may exclude much more besides.

That is the explanation of the fact that it is more presumptuous to order than to request. If you request you submit yourself to the addressee's judgment on the balance of reasons, while at the same time trying to add a reason on one side of that balance. But one who commands is not merely trying to change the balance by adding a reason for the action. He is also trying to create a situation in which the addressee will do wrong to act on the balance of reasons. He is replacing his authority for the addressee's judgment on the balance.

Similar considerations refute the second objection. There is a sense in which if one accepts the legitimacy of an authority one is committed to follow it blindly. One can be very watchful that it shall not overstep its authority and be sensitive to the presence of non-excluded considerations. But barring these possibilities one is to follow the authority regardless of one's view of the merits of the case (that is, blindly). One may form a view on the merits but so long as one follows the authority this is an academic exercise of no practical importance. We can go further than that and say that sometimes the very reasons that justify the setting up of an authority also justify following it blindly in a stronger sense—that is, following it without even attempting to form a judgment on the merits. This is the case, for example, with some traffic regulations. We all know the benefit from allowing traffic lights to regulate one's action rather than act on one's own judgment. But we tend to forget that a significant part of the benefit is that we give up attempting to form a judgment of our own. When I arrive at a red traffic light I stop without trying to calculate whether there is in the circumstances any reason to stop. From our vantage point we invented an example in which the question does not arise since the answer—there is no reason—is plain. But for the man in our example the question does arise; he has to discover whether there is no reason to stop. And if he is to inquire in this case he has to inquire in many other cases. For us it looks ridiculous to hear him say, "I am bound to follow authority regardless of the merits of the individual case," for we know in advance what the merits are and forget that he has to find that out, and not only now but in many other cases as well. Only when it is justified to prevent this is it also justified to accept authority in this respect, even if once in a while this makes one look ridiculous to the gods.

### Dissolving the Paradoxes

My last remarks in response to the objection to the simple view of authority help to explain both the force of the paradoxes and the way to overcome them. The paradoxes, I should hasten to say, pose no problem to the simple view of authority. On this view the commands of legitimate authority are facts of the world that are reasons for action. They are essentially like the weather and the stock exchange in being facts that are reasons for certain actions and against others. One no more abandons reason or forfeits one's autonomy if one follows the commands of authority than if one follows trends on the stock exchange.

This solution not only gets rid of the paradoxes but also presents them as simple and unforgivable mistakes. If, however, authority over persons is normative power over them, then we can explain the temptation that the paradoxes present without succumbing to it. I shall examine the paradoxes as presented by Robert Paul Wolff: "Men," he says "can forfeit their autonomy at will. That is to say, a man can decide to obey the commands of another without making any attempt to determine for himself whether what is commanded is good or wise."[24] Whatever the relevance of the second sentence to the problem of autonomy, it is true that accepting authority inevitably involves giving up one's right to act on one's judgment on the balance of reasons. It involves accepting an exclusionary reason.[25]

Wolff is anxious to emphasize that his view does not require people to disregard orders and commands altogether. The following shows both the strength and the weakness of his position.

For the autonomous man, there is no such thing, strictly speaking, as a command. If someone in my environment is issuing what are intended as commands, and if he or others expect those commands to be obeyed, that fact will be taken account of in my deliberations. I may decide that I ought to do what the person is commanding me to do, and it may even be that his issuing the command is the factor in the situation which makes it desirable for me to do so. For example, if I am on a sinking ship and the captain is giving orders for manning the lifeboats, and if everyone else is obeying the captain because he is the captain, I may decide that under the circumstances I had better do what he says, since the confusion caused by disobeying him would be generally harmful. But insofar as I make such a decision, I am not obeying his command; that is, I am not acknowledging him as having authority over me. I would make the same decision, for exactly the same reasons, if one of the passengers had started to issue "orders" and had, in the confusion, come to be obeyed.[26]

Wolff is making two valid and important points here. (1) Because an order is always given with the intention that it be taken as both an exclusionary reason and a first-order reason, its addressee has more options than either to disregard the order altogether or to obey it as he was intended to do. He may hold it to be a valid first-order reason, given the circumstances of its utterance, while denying that it is an exclusionary reason. (2) This means that an anarchist can reject the legitimacy of all authority while giving some weight to the instructions of de facto authorities. He can take such instructions to be first-order reasons without conceding the legitimacy of the authority. For it is only by acknowledging that such instructions are also valid exclusionary reasons that one accepts the legitimacy of the issuing authority. Only such an acknowledgment amounts to submission to authority for only it contains the necessary element of the denial of one's right to act on one's own judgment on the merits.

Reformulating Wolff's contentions in this way does show that there is more in them than simple confusions. He saw correctly that legitimate authority involves a denial of one's right to act on the merits of the case. But the reformulation also shows where he went wrong. He tacitly and correctly assumes that reason never justifies abandoning one's autonomy, that is, one's right and duty to act on one's judgment of what ought to be done, *all things considered.* I shall call this the principle of autonomy.[27] He also tacitly and wrongly assumes that this is identical with the false principle that there are no valid exclusionary reasons, that is, that one is never justified in not doing what ought to be done on the balance of first-order reasons. I shall call this the denial of authority.

This confusion is natural if one conceives of reasons as essentially first-order reasons and overlooks the possibility of the existence of second-order reasons. If all valid reasons are first-order reasons then it is a necessary truth that the principle of autonomy entails the denial of authority, for then what ought to be done all things considered is identical with what ought to be done on the balance of first-order reasons. But since there could in principle be valid second-order reasons, there is nothing in the principle of autonomy that requires the rejection of all authority.

The question of the legitimacy of authority takes the form that it was always assumed to take: an examination of the grounds that justify in certain circumstances regarding some utterances of certain persons as exclusionary reasons. There is no shortcut that will make such an inquiry redundant by showing that the very concept of legitimate authority is incompatible with our notion of rationality or morality.

### Notes

1. For a version of this principle of reason, see Davidson's principle of continence in his "How Is Weakness of the Will Possible" in *Moral Concepts,* ed. J. Feinberg (London: Oxford University Press, 1969).

2. This argument does not apply to theoretical authority. There is nothing immoral with having authorities on how to cook, program a computer, reduce money supply, and so on, but these are authorities upon what is theoretically the case. They can tell one how to do what one wants to do because they are aware of causal connections of which one may be unaware, but they can offer no help on the practical question of what to do. Submission to theoretical authority may, however, be irrational, for arguments about the conflict between authority and reason are not confined to practical authority.

3. They may be compatible with authority over small children and some mentally ill people.

4. Richard Tuck, "Why Is Authority Such a Problem?" in *Philosophy, Politics and Society,* 4th series, ed. P. Laslett, W. G. Runciman, and Quentin Skinner (Oxford: Blackwell, 1972).

5. My distinction between explanation in terms of types of justification and those in terms of types of actions justified is in itself problematic. Characterizing having authority as ability to perform actions justified by arguments of certain kinds is justificative explanation and not explanation as an ability to perform acts of a certain kind.

6. For a stimulating discussion of the notion of power as influence, see S. Lukes, *Power: A Radical View* (London: Macmillan, 1974).

7. It is sometimes defined as effective authority accepted by those subject to it or based on their consent. These facts, however, are relevant, if at all, only to the extent that they show the authority to be a justified one.

8. This should not lead one to confuse authority with the right to have authority. A person may be entitled to have authority and yet not have it: he may be entitled to it and entitled to have it conferred on him by Parliament and yet not have it until it is so conferred on him.

9. The use of expressions such as "according to law" is just one way of indicating that the statement is made from a point of view only. Often the context of utterance suffices to indicate this.

10. Robert Paul Wolff, *In Defense of Anarchism* (New York:

Harper and Row, 1970), p. 4.

11. John Lucas, *The Principles of Politics* (London: Oxford University Press, 1966), p. 16.

12. His definition confines the exercise of authority to the use of optatives. It seems that authority can also be exercised through nonverbal behavior and communication. But I am not concerned here with the examination of the different ways in which authority can be exercised.

13. A complete reason on this account is not necessarily one whose justification is self-evident. That I promised to perform a certain action is, I believe, a complete reason to perform it. But, of course, one may well be challenged to justify such beliefs and must be ready to justify them. One must defend, in other words, the belief that promises are reasons for actions. For further discussion of the presupposition underlying my use of "reasons" see *Practical Reason and Norms* (London: Hutchinson & Co., 1975), ch. 1.

14. Some requests, such as pleas and beggings, intend also to induce new spontaneous desires to accede to them. A "pure" request appeals to existing sympathies and to reason as sufficient to make it a reason for action for the addressee.

15. This statement has to be modified when orders in an institutionalized setting (such as the army) are involved. Cf. Peter Strawson, "Intention and Convention in Speech Acts," *The Philosophical Review* 73 (1964), 439-460. It should be remembered that I am not concerned with identifying acts of ordering, and so on, beyond what is necessary for my present purpose.

16. I am indebted for this objection to Philippa Foot and Kent Antley.

17. Further assumptions are required to show that I know that I have no reason to stop. For my purpose it is enough to establish that in fact I have no reason to stop. But in many situations these further assumptions obtain, and it is also true that for all I know there is no reason to stop.

18. I am assuming that he is entitled to make such an order—a matter that can be subject to dispute but that need not detain us here.

19. Cf. my "Voluntary Obligations and Normative Powers" in

*Proceedings of the Aristotelian Society,* Supp. Vol. 46 (1972): 79-102 and my *Practical Reason and Norms,* sec. 8, where the notion is more fully explained as well as given a more general definition. In this book, however, I erred in suggesting that a normative power is ability to change exclusionary reasons. Comments made by Philippa Foot forced me to realize that it is ability to change protected reasons (or exclusionary permissions). All mandatory rules are protected reasons.

20. This confusion undermines much of Richard Tuck's analysis in "Why Is Authority Such a Problem?"

21. Normally *X, Y,* and *Z* will be different persons. A person may, however, give authority to another to affect his own interests or give himself authority to affect the interests of another.

22. Advice differs from other cases of conveying information primarily in being given with the belief that it is or may be relevant to an actual or hypothetical question facing the recipient in his own estimate or in the opinion of the advisor and in being either intended by the advisor or expected by the recipient to be taken into account in the resolution of that practical problem.

23. This is not always an acceptable justification. Many legal orders, for example, are given with the intention that they shall be followed in the face of conclusive moral reasons against performing the ordered act. It may be that one should never regard such orders as binding and that no one has legitimate authority to issue such orders. But this in no way affects my point that such orders are often given. In the intention of the man giving the order it is to be taken as excluding even moral considerations.

24. Wolff, *In Defense of Anarchism,* p. 14.

25. Wolff is wrong in saying that accepting authority involves giving up the right or the attempt to form a judgment on the balance of reasons. Only action on that judgment is excluded (if it involves relying on excluded reasons which are not overridden).

26. Wolff, *In Defense of Anarchism,* pp. 15-16.

27. It is clear that this principle of autonomy is not really a moral principle but a principle of rationality.

# 3

# On legitimate authority: a reply to Joseph Raz[1]

**P. H. NOWELL-SMITH**

Dr. Raz makes two main claims: first, that he has given a correct analysis of the concept of authority, and second, that he can, armed with this analysis, show how it is that the paradoxes of authority are powerfully persuasive though ultimately illusory. I shall start with some critical comments on his first claim and then launch out into some methodological reflections prompted by, but not directly concerned with, his article.

## Raz's Analysis of Authority

Raz analyzes the concept of authority in terms of "normative power," which is, in turn, defined as *ability to change protected reasons for action.* He complains that Wolff's definition of authority is not perspicuous because it makes use of the concept of a right, which is "even more complex and problematic than that of authority." But to me it seems that the concepts of *ability* and of *reasons for action* are among the most problematic that we have.

I will start with "ability." There is, perhaps, a wide sense in which anyone who can speak "can" issue an order to anyone at any time. In this sense I can order Raz to leave the room right now. To this it might be replied that, while I can indeed utter certain words, there is a stronger sense in which I *cannot* give any such order. I should accept that reply; but it does point to the need for some analysis of the relevant sense of "ability," which seems to be the sense in which a pawn can only move forward or in which a colonel can give orders to a captain but not to a general. But if this is the sense of "can" that Raz has in mind, there is a clear danger of circularity in his definition. Moreover, this sense of "can" is characteristic of rule-governed institutions, and the concept of a rule is conspicuous by its absence from Raz's paper.

"The ability to change someone's reasons for action" seems much too wide a definition for "normative power" since it will ascribe normative power to anyone who wields a gun. What plainer case could there be of changing someone's reasons for action than pointing a gun at him while telling him to hand over his wallet? So Raz's account of authority seems not to meet even the first condition that any adequate analysis of authority must meet. It cannot capture the difference between the power of a gunman and that of someone whose imperative utterances are authoritative; and, indeed, it is the belief that this difference can never be captured that has led people to deny the existence of authority, to say that what we commonly call authority is really only naked power, so that to admit the existence of any authority is to deny reason or moral autonomy or both. But this extreme view suffers from the same defect as Mandeville's theory that Virtue is the Offspring that Flattery begot upon Pride. Just as no one could flatter our pride by calling us virtuous unless we already had a concept of virtue, so no one could ever profitably disguise his naked power as authority unless we already had a concept of authority. As Raz himself says, one requires authority to be *entitled* to command, and it is precisely the concept of *being entitled* that is puzzling and cannot be defined in terms of the ability to change people's reasons for doing things, since that is something that people can have without any title whatsoever.

## Reasons for Action

The phrase "reasons for action" is a term of art and in consequence is in need of explanation, the more so because it is currently enjoying a certain vogue. There is a sense in which someone has a reason for action even though he does not know it. If someone has left me a million dollars in his will, I have a reason for claiming it even if I am unaware of the legacy, and if there is a reckless drunk hurtling along just past that blind corner I have a reason for taking evasive action though I do not know that I have. But I do not think that these are the sorts of case that Raz has in mind, so I shall consider only that sense in which one speaks of "my reasons for doing something," and my reasons must be considerations that appeal to *me,* even if they are bad reasons or not really reasons at all.

Raz says nothing in a general way about "reasons for action" except, surprisingly, that $X$ has a reason to $\phi$ if and only if he ought to $\phi$. But rather than go into that, I will examine the distinction between first-order reasons and second-order exclusionary reasons, on which his claim to dissolve the paradoxes, while at the same time explaining their attraction, depends. What he says about this is, abstractly considered, clear enough. First, an order is intended by the speaker to provide a reason for action that supersedes whatever reasons for action the addressee may have when he considers the situation on its merits. Second, exclusionary reasons differ not in weight but in kind from first-order reasons. So far, so good. But when it comes to applying the distinction to an example I find some difficulties. My first methodological point is that most writers—and Raz is no exception—not only provide few examples but fail to present them in sufficient detail to bring out the crucial distinctions. Consider R. P. Wolff's example of the sinking ship. Raz does not give his own account of the example, but I think he means that on his account *also* it makes no difference whether it is the captain or someone else who is claiming authority. In both cases the orders are intended to provide exclusionary reasons and not to function as additional, and perhaps decisive, first-order reasons. So let us suppose that the captain and his officers are all drunk or in a panic; clearly no help is to be expected from them, and a mere passenger takes command. He starts issuing imperatives that others are beginning to obey. I obey him myself because I believe that following his lead is the only way to avert disaster, and one of the factors that leads me to make this decision is the fact that others are already following his lead.

I am not sure what Raz would say about the situation as so far described. He seems to suggest that the person who issues imperatives—whether the captain or a passenger—has authority and that, if I decide to follow his lead, I do so because I take his imperatives to be orders, that is, to provide me with second-order exclusionary reasons for doing what he says. But it seems clear that this is not so. If I decide to follow the lead of the other passenger, I make this decision on the merits of the case, even though my decision would have been a different one if others had not been following this passenger's lead. The fact that others are following is a decisive factor in the total situation, which I am judging on its merits.

But does it make any difference, for Raz, whether the imperatives are being issued by a passenger or by the captain? He might say that my account is correct in the case of the passenger. Being a mere passenger, he lacks authority, so his instructions can be only requests—requests with which I comply because the fact that others are already complying with them gives them a decisive weight that otherwise they would not have. On the other hand, if it is the captain, his instructions are authoritative orders. But if he takes this line, Raz will, I think, be forced into the position of having to distinguish between an (authoritative) order and a request in terms of the *de jure* status of the speaker, a position that he must find uncomfortable because of the ever-present spectre of circularity. (He has already rejected the attempt to distinguish between normative power and force in terms of a *right* to give orders.)

I shall return to this example because I think it can provide other important lessons; but to make my present point clear I shall consider a simpler example in which there is no doubt, from a common sense point of view, about the authority of the person giving orders. A rather diffident and slow-witted policeman is trying to sort out a traffic jam. I am a cool, clear-headed person, accustomed to command; I have a much better plan for sorting out the jam, and I know it. Should I do what the policeman tells me to do? And if so, why? Within certain limits—for example, the policeman has not given up altogether—I should do what he tells me. If I try to take command myself while the policeman is still giving orders, others will probably not follow my lead, and I shall get into a time-consuming discussion with the policeman. Thus I have good first-order reasons for doing what the policeman tells me to do. Given these factors in the situation, it is the best thing to do on the merits of the case. But have I also a second-order exclusionary reason for obeying the policeman? Certainly in a general way I recognize the authority of a traffic policeman to give me orders while according no such recognition to other citizens, however wise their advice or urgent their requests. But to recognize his authority is to recognize that he has a role under a system of rules under which I also have a role. His role entitles or requires him to give certain orders; my role, as a citizen, requires me to obey. It is the essence of a rule that it lays down who is required or permitted or forbidden to do what. Whether the existence of institutional rules of this kind gives rise even to a prima facie moral obligation to obey them is another matter.

Raz spells out the concept of giving an order solely in terms of the intentions of the speaker, not of the addressee, and in this example the speaker clearly intends me to take his utterances as providing me with an exclusionary reason. But whether he has the ability to change my reasons for action depends, surely, on whether I both recognize his intention (take his utterances as orders, not requests) and recognize his title to give such orders. In Austin's terminology, giving an order is an illocutionary act, but changing someone's reasons for action is perlocutionary.

If Raz is really to exorcise the paradoxes, he must explain more fully the distinction between "kind" and "weight" and show how one decides, or ought to decide, when a trivial authoritative order conflicts with a weighty request.

### Spellbound by Dichotomies

The basic question of political philosophy, a question that can be put in a variety of forms, is: Why, if at all, should I accept the right of another person or persons to tell me what to do? Its treatment has been bedeviled by crude dichotomies. For example, Wolff starts his discussion of authority in an entirely typical way: "Authority is the right to command, and correlatively, the right to be obeyed. It must be distinguished from power, which is the ability to compel compliance, either through the use or the threat of force." He goes on to give a clear example of power (the gunman) and a clear example of authority (the tax man). But what about the areas that are not so clear?

Consider again the example of the sinking ship. The captain and his officers have panicked, and a passenger takes charge. His posture, mien, coolness in a crisis, and commanding tone—perhaps he is a retired colonel who has not yet lost the habit of command—

contribute massively to the end result, that the passengers do what he tells them to do. Is he, in terms of Wolff's dichotomy, exercising authority or compelling compliance by the use of threat of force? Neither answer is appropriate to the situation. He is not in a position to use or to threaten force; the threat lies in the situation itself, and if he says, "Do as I say or you will drown," he is not threatening but predicting. But has he authority? If so, he must, according to Wolff, have a right to issue those crisp commands. How, then, does his status differ from that of a captain who, in a similar situation, has not panicked but is behaving precisely as does the passenger who takes command in the first case? In terms of Raz's distinction between normative power and sheer power (which is, I think, Wolff's "force"), do those features of his character and behavior to which I have drawn attention as contributing massively to the end result provide exclusionary reasons for others to obey him? It hardly seems so; yet it would totally misrepresent the situation to say that he merely advises or requests them to do what he says. If he had said, in a quiet and humble tone, "Please do as I ask; I think you will find, on reflection, that it is the only way to save your skins," would the other passengers have followed his lead? I think not.

Do those features of his tone and behavior provide reasons at all? There are some writers—and they are not only propagandists with axes to grind—who tell us that every way of getting someone to do something must be classified either as an appeal to reason or as violence. But this is only a particularly virulent form of dichotomitis of which the contrast between authority and force or the contrast between an order and a request are less virulent, but scarcely less lethal forms. What I hope that my example shows is that the ways in which one person can influence the behavior of another are manifold, that influence operates in subtle and complex ways and depends on subtle and complex factors. To ask whether a particular case is one of the exercise of authority is to ask too crude a question; often the only adequate reply would be that it had some of the features of a standard example of the exercise of authority and lacked others. Yet this answer suggests that there are standard cases; and if there are, it should be possible to give a rough delineation, not of necessary and sufficient conditions but of salient features. Perhaps the most instructive method would be to describe the standard case and then classify the various ways in which substandard cases can deviate from that norm.

## Linear Analysis and Understanding

At the root of every branch of philosophy we are apt to find a number, sometimes rather a small number, of concepts that seem to go along together; and one standard way of trying to get clear about these concepts and the relations between them is to try to define some of them in terms of others in a linear order so as to arrive at only one undefined term (if possible). This is the method that Raz adopts, and I do not doubt that, within limits, it is a useful one. It is certainly suitable for the construction of artificial systems, because we can operate an artificial system, like a calculus, without understanding its undefined terms—indeed I am not sure whether it even makes sense to talk of *understanding* the undefined terms of a calculus. But in a philosophical analysis—moving, for example, from the construction of logical systems to philosophical logic—the case is different.

Among the basic concepts of political philosophy are rights, obligations, duties, authority, and obedience. (Perhaps we should add states, sovereignty, and citizenship, but these seem less than universal.) I do not doubt that we can give rough accounts of some of these concepts in terms of others or that we can do this in many different ways, the choice between which is arbitrary, or that it may be helpful to do so. But this technique of linear analysis, used by itself, is bound to end in a dilemma: either we shall be left with an undefined concept within the group—in which case we shall have achieved no grasp of the whole—or we shall be tempted to define this undefined concept in terms of something outside the system, in which case we shall be rightly accused of reducing the entire vocabulary of politics to something that manifestly it is not. Examples abound. In the end Hobbes has to define "right" in terms of the sheer power of God who, he says, "by right, *that is* by absolute power commandeth all things"; and the cruder legal realists and positivists defined law as "the predictions of what the courts will decide" or "what officials do about disputes" or as the commands of someone habitually obeyed but not habitually obeying anyone else.

I am convinced that Professor H. L. A. Hart has a better method than this one. He invites us to take a close look at the manifold ways in which the terms of our moral and political vocabulary are actually used—in criticizing conduct, requiring justifications, admitting the validity of a criticism or a request for justification, and so on. Thereby he enables us to see that our use of normative vocabulary reflects styles of thought and action that cannot be reduced to or "analyzed in terms" of mere habits or power relations. To give but one example, an external observer who notices that when the lights turn from green to red most motorists stop and uses this information merely for predicting that they will in future do so, has not grasped what is meant by a *rule* and how the existence of a rule differs from the existence of a habit. Such an observer would not understand a rule-governed form of life.

This brings me to my next methodological point. The relation of "being a reason for" is nontransitive, a fact that is often overlooked because implication in logic is a transitive relation. If $X$ is a reason for $Y$ and $Y$ is a reason for $Z$, it does *not* follow that $X$ is a reason for $Z$. A simple example is found in a well-known, plausible, and perhaps even true theory about the justification for punishing someone.

According to this theory the justifying reason for having a system of criminal law—a system of commands plus threats—is that the system mimimizes antisocial conduct, and the justifying reason for punishing someone is that he has broken a law and thus incurred the penalty. This is a simple and familiar example of the distinction between the reason for having a rule and the reason for applying it, an example that highlights the nontransitivity of "being a reason for." It does not follow and is not always true that punishing someone will tend to minimize antisocial conduct. Now since *jus* is (very roughly) a system of rules, we may well find that a similar point about the nontransitivity of "being a reason for" may help us. It may well be the case that a valid reason for me to recognize the authority of an official over me is logically independent of any reason for recognizing the validity of the system of rules under which he has authority.

If this is right so far, the paradoxes can be readily resolved. The *de jure* authority of a policeman—what differentiates him from the gunman—is derived solely from the fact that he is entitled under the rules of the system to issue certain orders; and this could be the case even if the system itself were so monstrous as not to deserve our allegiance. But there is nothing at this point to make us say that to admit his authority must be to abandon either reason or autonomous morality. Still less is there any reason to say *at this point* that if an official of the system has any kind of authority at all to order me to do something wicked, his authority must be only de facto on the grounds that no authority can be *de jure* if his authority to give orders is contrary to the Moral Law (whatever that may be). Note that I am not saying that the mere fact that someone has *de jure* authority necessarily creates at least a prima facie reason for obeying him; for if the system is morally monstrous, it does no such thing. So I can recognize the *de jure* authority of a policeman without abandoning my moral autonomy. That he has *de jure* authority may be a plain matter of fact, and this is not to say that his authority, if he has any, is merely de facto. Failure to see this results from the fact that, outside philosophical discussions, those of us who are fortunate enough to live under more or less tolerable systems do recognize at least a prima facie moral obligation to obey the officials of our system. Hence anyone who says that the Lieutenant Governor of Ontario or a policeman has *de jure* authority may be assumed, in the absence of express denial, to accept the legitimacy of the system under which they have authority and thereby to admit at least a prima facie moral obligation to obey them.

The crux is found, of course, when we turn from the *de jure* authority of officials of a system to reasons for accepting the legitimacy of the system itself or recognizing the normative power to issue orders of persons who because they are at the top cannot derive their *de jure* authority within the system from someone else. Is it necessarily and always an abdication of rationality or moral autonomy to recognize a prima facie obligation to conform to the rules of a system, which include obeying its officials, when these rules have been made by someone else? Democrats have always assumed that it is, and that is why they have invoked patent fictions that purport to show that in obeying these officials I am really only obeying myself. But I do not think that the democrats are right or that these maneuvers are necessary. Here one must distinguish supreme from absolute or unlimited authority, concepts that tend to be confused whenever a claim to sovereignty is made. Ex hypothesi the sovereign person or body derives his title from no one else and is subject to no one's authority; but it is one thing to claim supremacy in this sense and quite another to claim that sovereign authority is absolute in the sense that all one's orders are to be obeyed. To recognize an absolute sovereign in this sense is indeed to abandon one's moral autonomy; for this means agreeing in advance that whatever first-order reasons—moral or prudential—I may have at some future time for $\phi$-ing are to be overborne by an order from the sovereign not to $\phi$.

Could it ever be rational to recognize absolute sovereignty? I am inclined to think that this would be rational if the state that claimed it were Plato's *Politeia* since, in that state, all orders given by the sovereign philosopher-kings are necessarily worthy of obedience. But this is academic speculation in the pejorative sense. To return to the paradoxes, I do not see that it is necessarily either irrational or immoral to recognize the moral legitimacy of a supreme authority; indeed there are some obvious and substantial reasons for so doing under certain conditions. What those conditions are is, of course, the main substantive question of political philosophy, and I certainly shall not attempt to spell them out here. Discussions of this question have all too often been confused by a failure to see that the reasons for recognizing supreme authority may be quite different from those for obeying a policeman. Perhaps they are connected, but not by such a simple relation as transitivity.

Raz has said that statements about the authority of an official in a particular system are relativistic; they are to be construed as expressing the belief that the official has authority in a nonrelativized sense, which remains to be analyzed. But although it is true that such statements are relative (to the system of rules), they cannot be construed as expressions of belief about some nonrelativized authority. What constitutes a foul in American football is not the same as what constitutes a foul in soccer. But this cannot be taken to mean that those who play American football believe that one may (in some absolute sense) pick up the ball and throw it while those who play soccer do not. If that were so, these football players would be contradicting each other. A legal system is not a game, but an analysis of authority under the rules in terms of beliefs about absolute authority is at best misleading. Consider the following case: an official has ordered $X$ to $\phi$ and $X$ consults his lawyer as to whether the order is within the official's authority. There are at least three replies that the lawyer might make.

1. Certainly; there's no doubt about it.
2. I believe it is, but I am not an expert in that branch of the law, and I shall have to look it up.
3. The regulation under which he claimed authority to give that order has not yet been tested in the courts; I believe it will be upheld, but one can never be sure.

It would be proper to call the second and third replies expressions of the lawyer's belief as to how the law stands in the relevant jurisdiction, as guarded assertions that that is how it stands; it would be clearly improper to call the first reply an expression of belief at all. Nor is it a confident and unguarded assertion to the effect that people in that jurisdiction believe that the official has unrelativized authority or to the effect that the courts in that jurisdiction will decide that he has if $X$ is prosecuted for disobedience. It is rather that in making this confident assertion as to how the law stands, the lawyer presupposes the nonrelativistic legitimacy of the system. The escape from relativism is not via Raz's translation of such statements into statements about people's beliefs but via Hart's distinction between statements made from the internal and those made from an external point of view.

## On Recognizing Authority

One can know what an apple is without knowing that apples are grown, bought, sold, cooked and eaten; but with the concept of authority this is not so. Authority can be granted, refused, claimed, exercised, recognized, denied, abused, flouted, aped, and so on. Together these activities constitute a *practice,* and once one has come to understand the practice as a whole, there is no further question as to what authority is. Moreover we cannot first come to know what authority is and then learn about the practice constituted by these activities, since there is nothing to understand apart from the activities.

In his analysis Raz leans too heavily on the point of view of one who has authority when he distinguishes giving an order, which is one way of exercising authority, from other imperative illocutionary acts such as advising and requesting. Authority, like loyalty, is a two-way street, especially when a dissolution of the paradoxes is attempted, since the paradoxes clearly arise from the point of view of the addressee. So I shall end by offering a sketchy transcendental argument to show that an analysis of authority in terms of the illocutionary act of ordering must also include an analysis of the concept of being ordered. There could be no such thing as ordering unless people in general (though not every person on every occasion) took certain utterances to be orders and understood the various responses that are conceptually open to one who takes an utterance addressed to him as intended to be an order.

The starting points of the argument are the concept of communication among rational men and Raz's definition of an order as an imperative uttered with the intention of its being taken by the addressee as an exclusionary reason for doing what is contained in the imperative. So our transcendental question is, How is it possible for someone to speak with the intention that the addressee take his utterance as an exclusionary reason for action? The argument proceeds as follows: As a rational man, $A$ can only say "$\phi$!" to $B$ with the intention that $B$ treat his utterance as an exclusionary reason for $\phi$-ing if he has reasonable grounds for believing that $B$ will so take it. But why should $B$ so take it? He will only take $A$'s utterance as an exclusionary reason for action if he recognizes $A$'s authority to provide him with such reasons. Hence, in a world in which addressees seldom or never took imperatives to provide exclusionary reasons but treated all imperative utterances as, say, requests, no rational man could address another in an imperative way with the intention that the addressee take his utterance to be an order. Unless there were a general practice of obedience (recognizing authority), there could not be a practice of giving orders. I am not trying to prove that rational men never indulge in speech acts that they know are hopeless; there are often good reasons for so doing. For example, I am a captain who has been ordered by the colonel to order a sergeant to $\phi$. I know very well that my insubordinate sergeant will disobey the order, but I pass it on just the same, to cover myself. Such cases are, however, necessarily parasitic on the existence of a *practice* of obedience to orders, and my transcendental argument is designed only to show that the existence of the practice, if it is dependent on the intentions of the speaker, must also be dependent on the recognition of the addressee.

### Note

1. Delivered at the colloquium. Some changes have been made by the editor to adjust to Dr. Raz's revisions.

# Part II.    EQUALITY

# 4

# Introduction

RICHARD BRONAUGH

There is controversy even about what to call it. The phrase "reverse discrimination" sometimes is charged with being a term of prejudice. On other occasions, it is deployed as a charge itself against purported wrongful instances of preferential hiring and admissions. Other times, the phrase is used neutrally for a social tendency that provides extra preference to otherwise unjustly disadvantaged persons or groups in a field of formally open competition. Trouble about the phrase suggests trouble with the idea.

All fair contests require criteria of relevance and a rule for winning. Marital status, sex, age, color, and national origin are recognizably irrelevant in most competitions, though not for the crown of Miss Teen-age Black America, should such a discriminating title exist. A just victory goes to someone on the basis of considerations grounded upon the settled point or purpose of competition. A widowed, elderly, white French-Canadian could not possibly lay any claim to the beauty title just mentioned; without looking at him one can see why. But logically speaking any fairly stable characteristic, such as being a left-handed redhead, could be relevant to some competition and required for victory. So there is no difficulty in recognizing that one of the purposes served by the law admissions board of the University of Texas in 1945, when the black man Sweatt applied, was racial segregation. Outlawing segregation forced a change of purpose, and Texas's wagon was unhitched from that misguided star.

Anyone who calls for the use of an *irrelevant* characteristic within any competition, therefore, is asking almost certainly for some new or expanded purpose to be recognized and for a change in the winning rule. Just as there was a purpose or policy goal served by excluding blacks from law school, so there can be a purpose or policy goal served by introducing "because he's black" as an active consideration to include a man in a law school class. Just as exclusion served racial segregation, so inclusion will serve racial integration. Someone who urges admission of a candidate because he is black has spoken relevantly or irrelevantly, it would appear, depending upon the purpose or policy served by the contest in question. Yet, on the other hand, one often hears that religion, nationality, marital status, sex, age, and color are all just "morally irrelevant pure and simple." If that is true, then a just society (or the pursuit of it) will establish no competitions based on policies that make these characteristics relevant. If such grounds are irrelevant, then no one can become eligible or ineligible upon them alone; they cannot even be used to break ties, for they are no reason for anything. Should this be the position one takes?

The problem that reverse discrimination presents comes about as follows. To put a ban upon policies that serve racial segregation is not automatically to promote racial integration. There is a difference between a prohibition and an affirmative measure. If no blacks apply to the law school, then racial segregation at the school continues in spite of the absence of a policy of discrimination. The situation so far is not difficult practically or morally; active recruitment of black applicants can be undertaken and candidates found. But then these applicants for the most part fail to compete successfully for the places in the class; they cannot succeed against the competition because of the winning rule in use. Their educational backgrounds are too deficient. At this juncture justice would seem to allow extra help; still, one must distinguish this from extra preference or preferential treatment. To give someone extra help is to provide him or her with tutors, financial aid, day-care facilities, and so on. Someone who has had extra help then applies and is judged against normal competitive criteria. But what if the policy goal of racial integration at the school is still not adequately served? To be given extra preference is a further affirmative step. The school introduces differential admissions standards for *sorts* of applicant. There still must be competition for admission among the members within the separate groups of applicant, but there is no direct competition among all the applicants taken together. Quotas are not automatically called for at this place, but they surely must tempt those who take the responsibility for the mix of the class. Quotas make it easy to explain how the decisions were reached, and the familiar meritarian winning rule probably continues to play a role, albeit within circumscribed subclasses of students. When quotas are set, it is quite obvious that there will be no competition between the membership of one class and the membership of another. The quota classifications themselves, of course, are drawn along standard racial, social, and biological lines; the number admitted will be a matter of controversy, though token quotas would be quick to spot. Thus classifications that were once struck down as "morally irrelevant pure and simple" become highly pertinent to the purpose of promoting racial integration, social or sexual equality, and so forth.

Two questions of social and political morality arise. First, is there anything wrong per se in using racial, social, and sexual classifications? Second, if they are not wrong, then is it ever right and mandatory that they be used? Everyone has a right that relevant considerations be used in deciding his or her distributive share of things scarce and valuable. Such classifications certainly will result in someone's being excluded from a school of law or medicine, but that is not as such a violation of rights; no one has an absolutely equal right to be placed in a professional school. As Professor Dworkin observes below, there is no equal right to go to law school as there is the equal right in a democracy to the vote. What of the right to equal consideration before the law? Here one would distinguish between the propriety of using any racial, social, or sexual classifications and the nature of the treatment one receives as a member of some class. The right to equal treatment appears to be the right to be considered with every other contestant equally before the winning rule and, therefore, a question of the nature of one's treatment within some class. Dworkin, however, conceives this right more broadly. The right becomes for him a thing also offended by purposes or policies that are reinforced by prejudice, in his phrase "by external preference," against one's race, sex, and so on. It is a right to equal protection, consideration, and treatment before the law, which is not, for instance, to be violated by a law school's admissions policy. Different professional schools will have special differing purposes, but all must be constrained by the right of an applicant not to be treated prejudicially. Dworkin's conclusion is that discrimination is not wrong when it serves morally proper goals, such as a more equal and integrated social order. But reverse discrimination is not right and mandatory as such. It is a matter of method; only on some occasions is it the instrumentality required.

Others have thought that preferential treatment is right and mandatory and not merely one acceptable method of affirmative action. It is said that justice demands it as compensation to victims of past wrongs. By way of contrast, consider a policy argument of the sort Dworkin finds acceptable. One argues that in a law school's admissions competition the winning rule has been framed upon purposes too narrowly conceived in the past. The usual meritarian criterion should be softened in recognition of the broad role always demanded of the graduates of this law school. The administration is to change the winning rule, or the subclasses in which it is applied, to enhance legal learning for the members of groups that rarely receive it and ultimately to bring them superior legal counsel and representation. This is a means to an end, and there are risks in this method. The group that needs improved legal attention may not be the best group from which to draw. If so, reverse discrimination would be a mistake. The end might be best achieved by selecting intellectually average whites with intense commitments to legal aid. But perhaps not in the long haul. Even if the best help is drawn from the group to receive it, education does make a difference to everyone's personality, prospects, and plans. Those admitted to law school for the reason that they are expected to return to the difficult environment from which they are drawn may come to regard the extra help and preference as a ticket to prosperity and freedom. But short of military-like contracts of service enforceable upon graduation, this is a normal risk. The nonreturner furthermore need not have forsaken the ghetto for self-serving reasons; schooling may expose an actual disability for the kind of practice demanded in a slum and reveal, in its place, academic brilliance. A selection committee acts on predictions. But disadvantaged groups might benefit from preferential treatment on the whole.

This argument, after the fashion suggested by Dworkin, is not grounded on considerations of compensation. To discuss that argument in the context of professional access, one must realize that the normal connection of such careers to affluence is not only a contingent matter but perhaps an injustice as well. So to discuss the problem, one assumes that there are no moral objections to the rewards typically attached to these careers. Now to adjust a winning rule by an argument for compensation owed past losers seems exceptionally weak and even dangerous. If a certain black woman, for instance, was excluded from a law school as black and female, though otherwise qualified, only she would be entitled to compensation for her unjust treatment. Since no one else could be entitled in a court of law to her compensation, the argument to support preferential treatment for groups of people is exceptionally weak. On the other hand, could it be that the right to receive compensation is passed along racial or sexual lines to other individuals and to future generations? Such a transfer might be explicable only upon assumptions shared with racists and sexists, so the argument is even dangerous. Yet it is not too difficult to understand the sense of saying that a general wrong has been enacted upon a group defined along certain familiar lines. What claim does any present member of that wronged group have against any present member of the historic group that committed the original wrong? One must distinguish the membership of disadvantaged groups from the membership of well-defined social and biological classes, not all of whom are victims of social injustice. These classes are not coextensive even though there is substantial overlap. Thus the class of those living at the subsistence level (for the reason of some injustice) cuts across all the usual classifications; even better-off groups cannot be easily captured in the usual classifications. Consider a black Canadian male who was raised in relative freedom from the harms of prejudice; should he, on moving to the United States, be entitled to preferential treatment at the hands of local institutions? The argument for preferred treatment as compensation owed to wronged groups will produce only rough justice.

# 5

# DeFunis and Sweatt*

## RONALD M. DWORKIN

### I

In 1945 a black man called Sweatt applied to the University of Texas
Law School but was refused admission because state law provided
that only whites could attend. The Supreme Court declared that this
law violated Sweatt's rights under the Fourteenth Amendment to
the United States Constitution, which provides that no state shall
deny any person the equal protection of its laws.[1] In 1971 a Jew
named DeFunis applied to the University of Washington Law
School; he was rejected although his test scores and college grades
were such that he would have been admitted if he had been black or
Filipino or a Chicano or an American Indian. DeFunis asked the
Supreme Court to declare that the Washington practice, which
offered less exacting standards to minority groups, violated his
rights under the Fourteenth Amendment as well.[2]

The Washington Law School's admissions procedures were
complex. Applications were divided into two groups. The majority—those not from the designated minority groups—were first
screened to eliminate all applicants whose predicted average, which
is a function of college grades and aptitude test scores, fell below a
certain level. Majority applicants who survived this initial process
were then placed in categories that received progressively more
careful consideration. Minority-group applications, on the other
hand, were not screened. Each received the most careful consideration, by a special committee consisting of a black law professor and
a white professor who had taught in programs to aid black law

---

*© 1977 by Ronald M. Dworkin. This chapter is essentially the same as Chapter 9,
"Reverse Discrimination," in Dworkin's *Taking Rights Seriously* (Cambridge,
Mass.: Harvard University Press, 1977). Reprinted by permission.

students. Most of the minority applicants who were accepted in the year in which DeFunis was rejected had predicted averages below the cut-off level for majority applicants. DeFunis's predicted average was well above the cut-off level, and the law school conceded that any minority applicant with his average would certainly have been accepted.

The *DeFunis* case split those political action groups that have traditionally supported liberal causes. The B'nai B'rith Anti-Defamation League and the AFL-CIO, for example, filed briefs as *amici curiae* in support of DeFunis's claim, while the American Hebrew Women's Council, the UAW, and UMWA filed briefs against it.

These differences among old allies demonstrated both the practical and the philosophical importance of the case. In the past liberals held, within one set of attitudes, three propositions: that racial classification is an evil, that every person has a right to an educational opportunity commensurate with his abilities, and that affirmative state action is proper to remedy the serious inequalities of American society. In the last decade, however, the opinion has grown that these three liberal propositions are in fact not compatible because the most effective programs of state action are those that give a competitive advantage to minority racial groups.

That opinion has, of course, been challenged. Many educators argue that benign quotas are ineffective; some argue that they are even self-defeating because preferential treatment will reinforce, not diminish, the sense of inferiority of minority races. But these are empirical judgments, and it is far too early, as wise critics concede, to decide whether preferential treatment does more harm or good. This empirical criticism is therefore reinforced by the moral argument that even if reverse discrimination does benefit minorities and does reduce inequalities associated with race, it is nevertheless wrong because distinctions of race are inherently unjust. They are unjust because they violate the rights of individual members of groups not so favored, who may thereby lose a place as DeFunis did.

DeFunis presented this moral argument, in the shape of a constitutional claim, to the courts. The Supreme Court did not, in the end, decide whether the argument was good or bad. DeFunis had, in fact, been admitted to the law school after one lower court had decided in his favor, and the law school said that he would be allowed to graduate however the case was finally decided. The Court therefore held that the case was moot and dismissed the appeal on that ground. But Mr. Justice Douglas disagreed with this neutral disposition of the case; he wrote a dissenting opinion in which he argued that the Court should have upheld DeFunis's claim on the merits. Many universities and colleges have taken Justice Douglas's opinion as handwriting on the wall, and are changing their practices already, in anticipation of a later Court decision in which his opinion prevails. In fact, his opinion pointed out that law schools might achieve much the same result by a more sophisticated policy than Washington used. A school might stipulate, for example, that applicants from all races and groups would be considered together, but that the aptitude tests of certain minority applicants would be graded differently, or given less weight in overall predicted average, because experience had shown that standard examinations were for different reasons a poorer test of the actual ability of these applicants. But this technique, if it is really meant to achieve the same result, is devious, and it remains to ask why the candid program the University of Washington used was either unjust or unconstitutional.

## II

Law school places are scarce and valuable. It makes a considerable difference to an individual applicant whether he is accepted by a good school. It also makes a great difference to the community which sorts of applicants law schools accept; it makes a difference whether they train bright students rather than rich ones, or public-spirited students rather than those who think only of their own careers. The decisions of admissions officers of law schools should be subject to a twofold test: they should respect the rights of individual applicants to fair treatment, and they should serve reasonable policy goals for the community as a whole.

That twofold test is, however, more complex than it might seem. The second branch requires that an admissions program be designed to make the community as a whole better in some particular way; there are a number of different sorts of policies that meet that test, and different law schools might choose different combinations or rankings of these. First, there are economic policies that aim to make the community better by allowing its members to have more of what they want. Improving the overall wealth of the community is an economic policy because an increase in community wealth improves the power of people, taken together, to purchase what they want. A law school might well design admissions criteria so as to admit students whose skills will improve commercial efficiency and therefore increase overall wealth. But economic policies include nonmonetary policies as well. If the community as a whole prefers clean air to the increased wealth that more industry would bring, then clear air is a nonmonetary economic policy. A law school might seek to advance that policy by trying to include, within its classes, some prospective lawyers who are concerned with environmental improvement.

Some policies are not economic at all, even in this wide sense. A law school might properly think that legal history is an important part of the community's culture, whether the community values it or not, and seek to preserve that discipline by admitting some future historians. In the same way, it might think that a more equal society is a more just society, whether the majority wants equality or not, and design its admission standards to advance the noneconomic goal of equality.

Reasonable people may differ, of course, as to which of these different economic and noneconomic policies is of superior importance. Each represents a different conception of the overall social good. Any particular law school may well pursue not one, but some combination, of policies. It may decide to take mainly the brightest students, because a more intelligent bar serves a variety of goals, and also to admit some less-intelligent applicants who have a special concern for the environment or for legal history or for social equality. Different schools will choose different combinations of such policies; the choice should be made, within the limits of rationality, by the schools themselves, not by the community as a whole through political decisions, nor by the courts through interpretation of the Constitution.

Law schools should not be free, however, to pursue even attractive policies at the expense of the rights of individual applicants who might be disadvantaged. Suppose the best law schools were to admit only members of the Republican party. That standard might indeed promote the economic goal of increased national wealth; but even if it did, it would be unjust and unconstitutional because it would punish the exercise of individual rights of political association and expression.

We might therefore restate the twofold test this way: a law school admissions scheme must be designed to promote some plausible conception of the collective good, whether economic or noneconomic, and it must choose means that respect individual rights. The traditional admission standards of American law schools seem to satisfy that twofold test. They are designed to choose, on the whole, the most intelligent applicants. That strategy improves the intellectual quality of the bar and therefore seems likely to promote a range of economic and noneconomic policies. It promotes these policies without compromising the rights of any individual, because no one has a right to be admitted to law school if he is less intelligent than others competing for the same places.

Did the special procedure the Washington Law School used for minority applicants meet the twofold test? It increased the number of minority students in the law school and therefore of minority lawyers in the community. That strategy might be thought to promote a number of economic policies. It might well improve the quality of legal education for all students, for example, to have a greater number of blacks as classroom discussants of social problems. If blacks are seen as successful law students, moreover, this might well encourage other blacks to apply who do meet the ordinary intellectual standards. That, in turn, would raise the intellectual quality of the bar. It is, as I said, controversial whether a preferential admissions program will in fact promote these economic policies, but it cannot be said to be implausible that it will. In any case such a program might more confidently be thought to serve the noneconomic policy of equality, because it should decrease the difference in wealth and power that now exists between different racial communities.

The Washington scheme therefore seems to pass the first test: it promises to serve a combination of attractive policies. But it would be wrong for the law school to serve these policies at the expense of individual rights. We must therefore ask as a second test, whether DeFunis had any rights so important that the law school must respect them even at the cost of policy.

He plainly had no absolute right that the state provide him a legal education of a certain quality, as he might, for example, have had a right that the state provide him shelter if he could not afford it himself. His rights would not have been violated if his state did not have a law school at all, or if it had a law school with so few places that he could not win one on intellectual merit. Nor did he have a right to insist that intelligence be the exclusive test of admission. Law schools use intelligence tests as standards for admission, not because applicants have a right to be judged in that way but to serve the various policies that an intelligent bar promotes. They sometimes serve these policies better, moreover, by supplementing intelligence tests with other sorts of standards; they sometimes prefer industrious applicants, for example, to those who are brighter but lazier. Law schools also serve noneconomic policies for which intelligence is much less relevant. The Washington Law School, for example, gave special preference not only to the minority applicants but to veterans who had been at the school before entering the military, and neither DeFunis nor any of the briefs submitted in his behalf complained of that preference.

So DeFunis did not have an absolute right to a law school place nor a right that only intelligence be used as a standard for admission. He said he nevertheless had a right that race *not* be used as a standard, no matter how well a racial classification might work to promote economic or noneconomic policies. He said he had this right by virtue of some more abstract legal right to equality protected by the Fourteenth Amendment to the Constitution, which provides that no state shall deny to any person the equal protection of the law. But the legal arguments made on both sides show that neither the text of the Constitution nor the prior decisions of the Supreme Court decisively settled the question of whether all racial classifications are unconstitutional. The Equal Protection Clause deploys the concept of equality as a test of legislation, but it does not lay down any particular conception of that concept.[3] Those who wrote the clause intended to attack certain consequences of slavery and racial prejudice, but it is unlikely that they intended to outlaw all racial classifications or that they expected that that would be the result of what they wrote. They outlawed whatever policies would violate equality and left it to others to decide what that means. There cannot be a good legal argument in favor of DeFunis, therefore, unless there is a good moral argument that all racial classifications violate some moral or political right to equality.

Can we find a good moral argument to that effect? We might begin by distinguishing two kinds of moral claims that an individual citizen might have to equality at the hands of government. The first is the right to *equal treatment,* which is the right to an equal distribution of some opportunity or resource or burden. Every person has a right to an equal vote in a democracy; that is the nerve of the Supreme Court's rule that one person must have one vote even if a different and more complex arrangement might better secure the collective welfare.

The second is the right to *treatment as an equal,* which is the right, not to receive the same distribution of some burden or benefit from the government, but to receive the same respect and concern in any calculation about how such benefits and burdens should be distributed. If I have two children, and one is dying from a disease that is making the other uncomfortable, I do not show equal concern if I flip a coin to decide which should have the remaining dose of a drug. This example shows that the right to treatment as an equal is fundamental and the right to equal treatment is derivative. In some circumstances the right to treatment as an equal will entail a right to equal treatment, but not, by any means, in all circumstances.

We have already decided that DeFunis did not have the first sort of right, the right to equal treatment in the assignment of law school places. He did not have a right to a place just because others were given places. He did have the second sort of right, that is, a right to treatment as an equal in the decision as to which admissions standards should be used. He had a right that his interests be treated as fully and sympathetically as the interests of any others when the law school decided whether to count race as a pertinent criterion for admission. But we must be careful not to overstate what that means. What follows from that right depends upon whether the law school is pursuing an economic or a noneconomic policy, or both.

Economic policies are designed to give the community as a whole what it prefers; the right to be treated as an equal is the right to have one's preferences counted in that calculation in the same way that the preferences of anyone else are counted. If a meritocratic admissions program is to be justified on economic policy, for example, the less intelligent applicants who will be refused have a right that their loss be counted in determining whether there is overall gain. But of course it does not follow that their loss, properly weighed, may not in fact be outweighed by gain to others. In the same way a program of minority preference, if it is to be justified on some economic policy, must respect the right of majority applicants to be treated as equals. Their losses must be counted in the calculation; but these losses may nevertheless be outweighed by gains to the community as a whole. If the Washington admissions process can be shown to serve a proper economic policy, then the fact that DeFunis was denied a place in consequence does not indicate, without more, that his right to be treated as an equal was compromised.[4]

Noneconomic policies, on the other hand, are justified by some conception of social virtue or justice taken to have independent value. A noneconomic policy is taken to be desirable even if the community as a whole does not prefer to have it. There can be no overriding requirement that an official relying on a noneconomic policy weigh the disadvantage to some against the gains to others, because he does not rely on any idea of overall gain to justify the policy. If objection is to be made to such a policy, it must be made either to the *merits* of the policy as such or to some *distinct* right of individuals, other than the right to treatment as an equal, that the policy violates. Suppose a law school believes that a society ruled by the rich is a nobler society just for that and so proposes to admit only rich applicants. We should object that that noneconomic policy is morally absurd because it finds no support in any plausible political morality. Suppose a law school believes that a society in which religion thrives is a better society, and so proposes to deny admission to atheists. Even if we did not think that policy absurd, we should still object that it violates an applicant's distinct right of religious liberty.

But DeFunis could not take objection to the noneconomic policy of improving social equality on grounds either that it lacked moral merit or that the means chosen to pursue it violated some distinct right. The policy of equality does find support in political morality, and the means chosen do not violate any distinct independent right like the right of religious freedom.[5]

So DeFunis's argument, taken as an argument of political theory, fails. He cannot object to the economic policies thought to be served by the Washington admissions scheme because they did not offend his right to be treated as an equal in the design of such policies. He cannot object to the noneconomic policy of equality served by that scheme because he cannot object to the merits of that policy or point to any independent right that the scheme dishonors. The Equal Protection Clause makes the concept of political equality a constitutional test of official decisions, but DeFunis cannot find in that concept any support for his claim that the clause makes all racial classifications illegal.

## III

If we dismiss DeFunis's claim in this straightforward way, however, we are left with this puzzle. How can so many able lawyers, who supported his claim both in morality and law, have made that mistake? These lawyers all agree that intelligence is a proper criterion for admission to law schools. They do not suppose that anyone's right to be treated as an equal is compromised by that criterion. Why do they deny that race, in the circumstances of this decade, may also be a proper criterion? They fear, perhaps, that racial criteria will be misused; that such criteria will serve as an excuse for prejudice against the minorities that are not favored, such as Jews. But that cannot explain their opposition. Any criteria may be misused, and in any case they think that racial criteria are wrong in principle and not simply open to abuse.

Why? The answer lies in their belief that, in theory as well as in practice, *DeFunis* and *Sweatt* must stand or fall together. They believe that it is illogical for liberals to condemn Texas for raising a color barrier against Sweatt and then applaud Washington for raising a color barrier against DeFunis. The difference between these two cases, they suppose, must be only the subjective preference of liberals for certain minorities now in fashion. If there is something wrong with racial classifications, then it must be something that is wrong with racial classifications as such, not just classifications that work against those in favor. That is the inarticulate premise behind the slogan, relied on by defenders of DeFunis, that the Constitution is color-blind. That slogan means, of course, just the opposite of what it says: it means that the Constitution is so sensitive to color that it makes any institutional racial classification invalid as a matter of law.

It is of the greatest importance, therefore, to test the assumption that *Sweatt* and *DeFunis* must stand or fall together. If that assumption is sound, then the straightforward argument against DeFunis must be fallacious after all, for no argument could convince us that segregation of the sort practiced against Sweatt is justifiable. Superficially, moreover, the arguments against DeFunis do indeed seem available against Sweatt, because we can construct arguments of economic policy that Texas might have used to justify its program of segregation.

Suppose the Texas admissions committee, though composed of men and women who themselves held no prejudice, decided that the Texas economy demanded more white lawyers than they could educate, but could find no use for black lawyers at all. That might have been, after all, a realistic assessment of the commercial market for lawyers in Texas just after World War II. Corporate law firms needed lawyers to serve booming business but could not afford to hire black lawyers, however skillful, because the firms' practices would be destroyed if they did. It was no doubt true that the black community in Texas had great need of skillful lawyers and would have preferred to use black lawyers if these were available. But the committee might well have thought that the commercial needs of the state as a whole outweighed that special need.

Or suppose the committee judged, no doubt accurately, that alumni gifts to the law school would fall off drastically if it admitted a black student. The committee might deplore that fact, but nevertheless believe that the consequent collective damage would be greater than the damage to black candidates (and the black community) excluded by the racial restriction.

It may be said that these hypothetical arguments are disingenuous because any policy of excluding blacks would in fact be supported by a distaste for blacks as such, and arguments of this sort would be rationalization only. But if these arguments are sound as arguments of economic policy, they might be accepted by people who do not have the prejudices the objection assumes. It therefore does not follow from the fact that the admissions officers were prejudiced, if they were, that they would have rejected these arguments if they had not been. If the objection supposes that applicants to a law school have a right to be considered by men and women who in fact have no prejudices of any sort, it plainly goes too far, for there are very few such people. If it means that they have a right that those who judge them not take their prejudices into account, then this right will be satisfied if the prejudice is so deep and automatic that it is unconscious.

In any case, arguments like those I describe were in fact used by officials who might have been free from prejudice against those they excluded. Decades ago, as the late Professor Alexander Bickel reminds us in his brief for the B'nai B'rith, President Lowell of Harvard University argued in favor of a quota limiting the number of Jews who might be accepted by his university. He said that if Jews were accepted in numbers larger than their proportion of the population, as they certainly would have been if intelligence were the only test, then Harvard would no longer be able to provide men of the qualities and temperament it aimed to produce—men, that is, who were more well-rounded and less exclusively intellectual than Jews tended to be, and who, therefore, were better and more likely leaders of other men, both in and out of government. It was no doubt true, when Lowell spoke, that Jews were less likely to occupy important places in government or at the heads of large public companies. If Harvard wished to serve some economic policy by improving the intellectual and social qualities of the nation's leaders, it was rational not to allow its classes to be filled up with Jews. The men who reached that conclusion might well prefer the company of charming and erudite Jews to that of the Wasps who were more likely to become senators. Lowell suggested he did, though perhaps the responsibilities of his office prevented him from frequently indulging his preference.

It might now be said, however, that discrimination against

blacks, even when it does serve some plausible economic policy, is nevertheless unjustified because it is invidious and insulting. The briefs opposing DeFunis make just that argument to distinguish his claim from Sweatt's. Because blacks were the victims of slavery and legal segregation, they say, any discrimination that excludes blacks will be taken as insulting by them, whatever arguments of economic policy might be made in its support. But we must be careful to distinguish the question of whether some social arrangement is taken as insulting by a particular group from the different question of whether it is in fact insulting to them. It seems wrong, and retrograde, to make constitutional judgments turn on popular misperceptions. If segregation does serve some proper economic policy, even when the loss to blacks is counted against the overall gain, then the fact of segregation, without more, is not insulting to blacks, any more than discrimination against the less intelligent is insulting to them. Sweatt's belief that the arrangement insults him would then be a mistake, and though his mistake would be historically explicable, we should not allow it to disqualify the arrangement. If we do, then we simply perpetuate an unfortunate misperception that is by hypothesis harmful to the general welfare; if, instead, we proceed with the arrangement, explaining our grounds as carefully as we can, then we attack the unfortunate and expensive belief that discrimination is the same as insult.

It would be wrong, in any case, to assume that men in the position of DeFunis will not take *their* exclusion to be insulting. They are very likely to think of themselves not as members of some large majority group that is privileged overall, but as members of some other minority, like Jews or Poles or Italians, whom comfortable and successful liberals are willing to sacrifice in order to delay more violent social change. If we wish to distinguish *DeFunis* and *Sweatt* on some argument that uses the concept of an insult, we must show that the treatment of the one, but not the other, is in fact insulting (unjust), not merely that it is taken as an insult.

## IV

So these familiar arguments that might distinguish the two cases are unconvincing. That seems to confirm the view that Sweatt and

DeFunis must be treated alike and therefore that racial classification must be outlawed altogether. But fortunately a more successful ground of distinction can be found to support our initial sense that the cases are in fact very different. This distinction does not rely, as these unconvincing arguments do, on features peculiar to issues of race or segregation or even on features peculiar to issues of educational opportunity. It relies instead on further analysis of the general idea and appeal of economic policies.

The arguments I invented for Texas to use against Sweatt are all economic arguments: they hold that if the state law school is segregated, the community will be better off overall because more of the people will have more of what they want. Plainly the idea of an economic policy that allows losses to some citizens to be set off against gains to others requires some account of how these losses and gains are to be measured and compared. Some philosophers and economists deny that any such measurement or comparison is possible. They therefore think that economic policies must be confined to policies that make some one better off and no one worse off, which are rare and trivial, or to policies that increase the aggregate monetary wealth of the community as a whole, without regard to distribution, which are often unjust. These constraints sharply reduce either the usefulness or the appeal of economic policies.

In practice, officials do make welfare comparisons that set off gains to some against losses to others, and there are two theories in the field about how these comparisons should be made. The first is Bentham's theory of psychological utilitarianism. Bentham thought that political officials should be able, at least in principle, to calculate the pleasure or pain that a particular policy would bring to different groups of citizens. In Benthamite theory, the claim that segregation advances policy is simply the claim that segregation produces an improved balance of pleasure overall. In his phrase, it promotes the greatest good of the greatest number.

It is a standing objection to psychological utilitarianism, however, that in fact officials have no way of identifying the subjective quality of pleasure or pain that any individual or group feels. Any judgment about the aggregate of pleasure and pain that segregation produces within a large community can be only a wild guess. Those who make this objection to Bentham propose a different version of utilitarianism. They ask officials to determine the preferences of the individual members of the community by noticing how much each individual is willing to pay for a particular benefit or how much of some other benefit he is willing to sacrifice for it, or how much he is willing to use of his voting or other political power to have it. An official might then choose the policy that achieves the best possible satisfaction of all these different preferences, taking into account their strength as well as their distribution. If a great many people strongly prefer the consequences of segregation, then these preferences might well outweigh, on balance, the preferences of the many fewer people, like Sweatt, who do not.

Preference utilitarianism does require that officials compare the strength and number of the different preferences that different members of the community have, and those philosophers and economists I mentioned who believe that no such comparisons can be made objectively reject preference utilitarianism as well as psychological utilitarianism for that reason. It is nevertheless more plausible to compare the relative strength of preferences, as these are revealed in the marketplace and in politics, than to compare relative degrees of subjective pleasure, and preference utilitarianism is now much more popular than psychological utilitarianism: it is, I think, the working political theory of a great many actual political officials. I shall discuss utilitarianism with preference utilitarianism in mind, but my discussion would hold for psychological utilitarianism as well.

Utilitarianism in either form has considerable egalitarian appeal because of its apparent impartiality. If the community has only enough medicine to treat some of those who are ill, utilitarianism holds that those who are most ill should be treated first. If the community can afford a sports stadium or an opera house, but not both, and more people want the stadium, then utilitarianism holds that the community ought to build that, unless the opera lovers can show that their preferences are so much more intense that taken together they have more weight in spite of the numbers. One sick man is not to be preferred to another because he is worthier of official concern; the tastes of the opera lover are not to be preferred because they are more admirable. These examples suggest that utilitarianism not only respects but embodies the right of each citizen to be treated as the equal of any other. The chance that each individual's preferences have to succeed, in the design of economic policy, will depend upon the intensity of that preference, balanced against the parallel or competing preferences of others. His chance will not be affected by the esteem or contempt of either officials or fellow citizens, and he will therefore not be subservient or beholden to them. Utilitarianism seems to provide, therefore, not only a method for measuring gains and losses so as to determine economic policies but a reason for supposing that economic policies are fair. It seems to provide a philosophical basis for the statement made earlier that though economic policy may justify very unequal treatment of different citizens, it nevertheless respects their rights to be treated as equal, that is as equal and independent members of civil society.

But the simple examples that suggest that comfortable conclusion are misleading, however. Utilitarianism assumes that the preferences individual citizens have, which a utilitarian calculation must take into account, are preferences for one social state of affairs over another, that is, for one full distribution of goods and opportunities over another. That assumption is in fact made explicit in the theoretical writing of distinguished welfare economists, like Kenneth Arrow. But if that is so, then an individual's overall preference, as revealed in his market or political behavior, may express, on further analysis, either a personal preference for his own enjoyment of some goods or opportunities or an external preference as to how goods or opportunities should be distributed among everyone else, or both. If external preferences are counted along with personal preferences, then the egalitarian character of utilitarianism is corrupted because the chance that anyone's preferences have to succeed will then depend not only on the demands that the personal preferences of others make on scarce resources but on the respect or affection they have for him or for his way of life.

This corruption is plain when some people have external preferences because they hold political theories that are themselves contrary to utilitarianism. Suppose many citizens, who are not themselves sick, are racists in political theory and therefore prefer that scarce medicine be distributed first to the white man rather than the sicker black man. If utilitarianism counts these political preferences at face value, then it will be, from the standpoint of personal preferences, self-defeating, because the distribution of medicine will then not be utilitarian at all. In any case, self-defeating or not, the distribution will not be egalitarian in the sense defined. Blacks will suffer, to a degree that depends upon the strength of the racist preference, from the fact that others think them less worthy of respect and concern.

There is a similar corruption when the external preferences that are counted are altruistic or moralistic. Suppose many citizens, who themselves have no taste for opera, prefer the opera house to be built because they are specially concerned about the welfare of opera lovers, or because they think that sports watching is immoral and ought to be repressed. If the altruistic preferences are counted, so as to reinforce the personal preferences of opera lovers, the result will be a form of double counting: each opera lover will have the benefit not only of his own vote, but also of the vote of someone else who takes pleasure in his success. If the moralistic preferences are counted, the effect will be the same: sports lovers will suffer because their preferences are held in lower respect by those whose personal preferences are not themselves engaged.

In these examples, external preferences are independent of personal preferences. But of course political, altruistic, and moralistic preferences are often not independent but are grafted on to the personal preferences they reinforce. If I am white and sick, I may also hold a racist political theory. If I want an opera house for my own enjoyment, I may also be altruistic in favor of my fellow opera lovers, or I may also think that sports watching is immoral. The consequences of counting these external preferences will be as grave for equality as if they were independent of personal preference, because those against whom the external preferences run might be unable or unwilling to develop reciprocal external preferences that would right the balance.

External preferences therefore present a great difficulty for utilitarianism. That theory owes much of its popularity to the assumption that it embodies the right of citizens to be treated as equals. But if external preferences are counted in overall preferences, then this assumption is jeopardized. That is, in itself, an important and neglected point in political theory; it bears, for example, on the liberal thesis, first made prominent by John Stuart Mill, that the government has no right to enforce popular morality at law. It is often said that this liberal thesis is inconsistent with utilitarianism because if the preferences of the majority that homosexuality should be repressed, for example, are sufficiently strong, utilitarianism must give way to their wishes. But the preference against homosexuality is an external preference, and the present argument provides a general reason why utilitarians should not count external preferences of any form. If utilitarianism is suitably reconstituted so as to count only personal preferences, then the liberal thesis is a consequence, not an enemy, of that theory.

It is not, however, a simple matter to reconstitute utilitarianism so as to count only personal preferences. Sometimes personal and external preferences are so inextricably tied together and so mutually dependent that no practical test for measuring preferences will be able to discriminate the personal and external elements in any overall revealed preference. When that is so, the utilitarian who takes seriously the right of individuals to be treated as equals must make the following choice. If he judges that whatever external preferences might corrupt his calculation are weak or randomly distributed—if he judges, for example, that only a small part of the population thinks that sports watching is immoral—then he may discount the influence of these external preferences altogether and take overall revealed preferences at face value. But if he judges otherwise—if, for example, sports watchers form a distinct and traditionally disliked minority—then he cannot accept as fair any utilitarian argument of economic policy purporting to justify a disadvantage to that minority.

We may now bring this abstract discussion of utilitarianism to bear on racial segregation. The preferences that might justify the University of Texas's program of segregation on grounds of economic policy are either external or are inextricably combined with and dependent upon external preferences. That is certainly true of the preference of white students for white classmates, of white businessmen to employ white lawyers, and of white alumni to donate to an all-white school. Most of those who have these overall preferences either hold political theories according to which whites are entitled to more official respect and concern than blacks or care more for the welfare of whites than blacks or believe that institutions that throw whites and blacks together are immoral. These political, altruistic, and moralistic preferences are in fact so widespread that they corrupt any argument of economic policy in favor of segregation.

I concede that some of those who favor segregation would say that they hold no such external preference; they say that they dislike the company of blacks simply as a matter of personal preference and not as a matter of political, social, or moral theory. It is worth noticing, however, that once a distinction between personal and external preferences is recognized, these associational preferences can no longer be regarded as purely personal. Some of an individual's personal preferences, like having a legal education, can be satisfied by society only through institutions such that his preferences must be satisfied in company with others of similar preference. If he has a preference to attend law school with whites rather than blacks, then his preference is at once a personal preference and an external preference about how institutional opportunities created in part to satisfy him shall be distributed to others. If associational preferences are counted in a utilitarian calculation, and these run against a particular racial group, then the egalitarian character of the calculation will be corrupted just as if political or altruistic or moralistic preferences are counted. If Texas seizes on any of these external preferences in order to justify segregation as economic policy, then the competing personal preferences of blacks have been counted in the balance at a discount. Blacks are denied their right to be treated as equals because the chance that their preferences will prevail is heavily reduced by the low esteem in which others hold them.

It does not matter, to this conclusion, whether these external preferences figure directly or indirectly in the utilitarian calculation. Suppose Texas justifies segregation by pointing to the apparently neutral economic policy of increasing community wealth, which satisfies the personal preferences of everyone for better homes, food, and recreation. If the argument that segregation will improve community wealth depends upon even the *fact* of external preferences: if the argument notices, for example, that because of prejudice industry will run more efficiently if factories are segregated, then the argument has the consequence that the black man's personal preferences are defeated by what others think of him. Utilitarian arguments that justify a disadvantage to members of a race against whom prejudice runs will always be unfair arguments unless it can be shown that the same disadvantage would have been justified in the absence of the prejudice. If the prejudice is widespread and pervasive, as in fact it is in the case of blacks, that can never be shown. The preferences on which any economic policy justifying segregation will be based will be so intertwined with prejudice that they cannot be disentangled to the degree necessary to make any such contrary-to-fact hypothesis plausible.

We now have an explanation that shows why segregation that disadvantages blacks is, in the United States, an automatic insult to them and why such segregation offends their right to be treated as equals. The argument confirms our sense that economic arguments purporting to justify segregation are not simply wrong in detail but misplaced in principle. This form of objection to economic policy is not, however, limited to race or even prejudice. There are other examples of external preferences that might offend the rights of citizens to be treated as equals and it is worth noticing these briefly, if only to protect the argument against the charge that it is constructed ad hoc for the racial case. I might have a moralistic preference against professional women, or an associational preference for pretty girls, or an altruistic preference for virtuous men. It would be unfair for any law school to count preferences like these in deciding whom to admit to law schools; unfair because these preferences, like racial prejudices, make the success of personal preferences of a man or woman depend on the esteem and approval, rather than on the competing personal preferences, of others.

The same argument does not hold, however, against an economic policy used to justify admission based on intelligence. That policy need not rely, directly or indirectly, upon the preferences of the community for the company of intelligent rather than dull lawyers or any community sense that intelligent lawyers are intrinsically more worthy of respect. It relies instead upon the law school's own judgment, right or wrong, that intelligent lawyers are more effective in satisfying personal preferences of others, like the preference for wealth or winning law suits. It is true that law firms and clients prefer the services of intelligent lawyers; that fact might make us suspicious of any economic argument that is said not to depend upon that preference, just as we are suspicious of any argument justifying segregation that is said not to depend upon prejudice. But the widespread preference for intelligent lawyers is, by and large, an instrumental rather than an associational preference: law firms and clients prefer intelligent lawyers because they believe that such lawyers will be more effective in serving their personal preferences. Kant distinguished treating another person as a means from treating him as an end. The preference for intelligent lawyers is instrumental because it treats them as a means to independent goals; the preference for white lawyers is associational because it values the society of whites, and denigrates the society of blacks, as an end in itself. Instrumental preferences of that character do not themselves figure in utilitarian arguments of economic policy, though a law school may accept, on its own responsibility, the instrumental hypotheses upon which such preferences depend.[6]

## V

We therefore have the distinctions in hand necessary to distinguish *DeFunis* from *Sweatt*. The arguments in favor of refusing to admit any blacks to law school are all economic arguments, and they are all economic arguments that rely upon external preferences in such a way as to offend the rights of black citizens to be treated as equals. The arguments in favor of an admissions program that discriminates in favor of blacks are both economic and noneconomic. Some of the economic arguments do rely, at least indirectly, on external preferences (such as the preference of certain blacks for lawyers of their own race); but the economic arguments that do not rely on such preferences are strong and may be sufficient. The noneconomic arguments rely not upon preferences but on the independent argument that a more equal society is a better society, even if its citizens prefer inequality. That argument does not deny anyone's right to be treated as an equal himself.

We are therefore left, in *DeFunis,* with the simple and straightforward argument with which we began. Racial criteria are not necessarily the right standards for deciding which applicants should be accepted by law schools. But neither are intellectual criteria nor, indeed, any other set of criteria. The fairness of any admissions program must be tested in the same way. It is justified if it serves a proper policy that respects the right of all members of the community to be treated as equals, but not otherwise. The criteria used by schools that refused to consider blacks failed that test, but the criteria used by Washington do not.

We are all rightly suspicious of racial classifications. They have been used to deny, rather than to respect the right of equality, and we are all conscious of the consequent injustice. But if we misunderstand the nature of that injustice because we do not make the simple distinctions that are necessary to understand it, then we are in danger of more injustice still. It may be that preferential admissions programs will not in fact make a more equal society because they will not have the effects their advocates believe they will. That strategic question should be at the center of debate by supposing that these programs are unfair even if they do work. We must take care not to use the Equal Protection Clause to cheat ourselves of equality.

### Notes

1. *Sweatt* v. *Painter*, 339 U.S. 629, 70 S.Ct. 848.
2. *DeFunis* v. *Odgaard*, 94 S.Ct. 1704 (1974).
3. See "Nixon's Jurisprudence," *New York Review of Books,* May 4, 1972.
4. I do not mean to suggest that an individual may never object to an economic policy if his losses are outweighed by gains to others. He may certainly object if, under the peculiar circumstances, he has not only a right to be treated as an equal but a right to equal treatment. Suppose some state does not admit children of low intelligence to its elementary schools. It urges that the money necessary to educate such children is more efficiently spent providing a better education for the more intelligent. We might well say that since someone who does not have an elementary education is unable to lead a useful life, individuals have a right to equal treatment in any provision for such

education. If so, this educational program would violate the rights of the children excluded, even if these children were so few that their losses would in fact be outweighed, in some economic calculation, by the total gains to the large majority. But law school education is not so vital to prospects for life that every applicant has an equal right to be admitted.

5. DeFunis did not claim that his right not to have race used as a criterion is a distinct right like the right to religious liberty. He claimed that that right follows from the more general right to treatment as an equal. He cannot now urge its independent standing in support of that claim, nor could he defend that independent standing if he did wish to claim it.

6. No doubt the preference that some men and women have for intellectual companions is associational; they value these companions not as a means to anything else but as an end in itself. If such preferences were sufficiently strong and pervasive, we might reach the same conclusion here that we reached about segregation, that is, that no economic policy that discriminates against less intelligent men and women as such could be trusted to be fair. But there is no reason to assume that the United States is that intellectualistic, certainly no reason to think that it is intellectualistic to a degree that it is racist.

# 6
# Rights, utility, and racial discrimination
## DAVID LYONS

State law barred Sweatt from the University of Texas Law School because he was black, and the Supreme Court's finding that he was subjected to wrongful discrimination was generally applauded. DeFunis was rejected by the University of Washington Law School under a policy of reverse discrimination: applicants from minority groups who had credentials similar to his would have been accepted. Was that wrongful too? Many assume that these two cases stand or fall together, but Professor Dworkin claims that they are different.

It can be argued that reverse discrimination serves "reasonable policy goals," such as equality or the general welfare, but to be justified, Dworkin maintains, it must also respect individual rights. Dworkin argues that DeFunis's rights were not violated. DeFunis had no relevant right to equal treatment (admission if anyone else gets in), for example, though he had the right to treatment as an equal (that is, to equal consideration), and the latter was presumably respected when losses such as his were taken into account. That suggests reverse discrimination might be justified. But, Dworkin notes, it could also be argued that discrimination of the sort practiced against Sweatt served reasonable policy goals, under the circumstances that then prevailed. And Sweatt, too, had no right to law school admission, as such. How, then, can we differentiate between the cases? Dworkin seems to say: only by showing that Sweatt's right to be treated as an equal—to be given equal consideration—was violated even though DeFunis's was not.

Dworkin's article has a twist that merits special notice. The arguments that might be used against Sweatt are all "economic," or utilitarian, designed to show that the segregation policy will give more people more of what they want. But the interests that work this way are basically "external preferences," concerning how others should be treated, such as the desire of a white majority to discriminate against blacks. Now, Dworkin maintains, much of the appeal of utilitarianism lies in its apparent impartiality, its counting each for one and none for more than one, its embodiment of the right to equal consideration, even when it does not mandate equal treatment. But this egalitarian aura disappears once we recognize the consequences of accommodating external preferences. It is not just that the results are morally objectionable. Allowing utilitarian calculations to be swayed by external preferences permits some persons' preferences to be inflated while others' are discounted (white racists and black victims, respectively, in the case of a white majority's strong preference for white supremacy).

Dworkin seems to conclude that we must reject all arguments that turn upon external preferences. This is not presented as a simple rejection of utilitarianism. Dworkin supposes that its sympathizers are more fundamentally committed to equal consideration and will wish to restrict utilitarian calculations accordingly. If we do reject the corresponding economic arguments, we shall respect this right and at the same time distinguish *DeFunis* from *Sweatt* even within the limits of utilitarianism (suitably refined), for racist discrimination turns entirely on such arguments, while reverse discrimination does not.

Dworkin thus employs the right to equal consideration to distinguish *DeFunis* from *Sweatt,* but his primary concern (beyond these cases) is with clarifying the relations between such rights and legitimate social goals, such as the utilitarian goal of getting people more of what they want.

The distinction Dworkin draws between *DeFunis* and *Sweatt* may seem sharper than it really is because Dworkin says that legitimate social goals may not violate individual rights. This seems to imply that *any* right outranks *any* argument grounded on utility (or other social goals) and thus that reverse discrimination (assuming it violates no rights) might be justified (that depends on its relation to such goals) while discrimination of the sort practiced against Sweatt could not be justified.

But this is an illusion. The principle, so understood, is overstated, as Dworkin himself would seem to agree. He suggests his reservations here when he asks "whether DeFunis had any rights *so important* that the law school must respect them even at the cost of policy."[1] The qualified position is developed in Dworkin's paper, "Taking Rights Seriously," where he argues that rights must make a substantive difference in our calculations; they cannot be outweighed by merely minimal or marginal utilities. But they can be overridden, not just by other rights but also by considerations of what I would call utility, for example, "to prevent a catastrophe, or even to obtain a clear and major public benefit."[2]

But if considerations of utility can sometimes outweigh rights, then they are always relevant, and Dworkin's distinction between *DeFunis* and *Sweatt* is not practically decisive. In order to determine what to do, we must consider the utilities involved. As Dworkin would no doubt agree, his distinction does not justify reverse discrimination since great disutilities (or other evils) may result. I am not so sure, however, that he would willingly accept the following point: great utilities might justify the sort of discrimination practiced against Sweatt. If we are guided by the more plausible version of Dworkin's principle, we cannot assume that such discrimination cannot be justified just because it violates a right.

In "Taking Rights Seriously," however, Dworkin also suggests that certain rights, which he calls "fundamental," cannot justifiably be violated merely for the sake of extra benefits, even if major.[3] He might accordingly object here by saying that the right to treatment as an equal is fundamental. This argument would resharpen the distinction between *DeFunis* and *Sweatt*. But before we allow ourselves to accept this possibly congenial position, we should observe that no argument has been given for the right to be treated as an equal or the idea that it (or any right) must be respected at all costs—that nothing could possibly justify its violation. In the absence of such arguments, the distinction seems to dull perceptibly.

Once its sharpness is called into question, it seems incumbent on us to ask whether a comparably secure distinction between *DeFunis* and *Sweatt* could be made on utilitarian grounds. Dworkin seems, in effect, to deny this. He does not say so, but his denial seems assumed by his strategy of invoking rights to equal consideration. But why should he suppose this? Surely it cannot be thought that the mere possibility of "plausible" arguments for racist as well as for reverse discrimination shows that they cannot soundly be distinguished on utilitarian grounds, for the overall utilities may *in fact* be lopsided, favoring *Sweatt* but not *DeFunis*.

Dworkin might be taken as suggesting that utilitarian arguments cannot possibly account for the distinction because they simply weigh advantages and disadvantages on one side and the other. Dworkin might be seen as saying that there is a *qualitative* difference between the cases, indicated by the rights involved, which utilitarianism can only obscure. It may also be said that unrestricted utilitarianism is shown to be defective here simply because racist attitudes are allowed to carry weight in its calculations and that this applies even if overall utility calculations always in fact reject racism. But to criticize utilitarianism on such grounds alone simply begs the question, assuming that the moral point is independent of utilities. Much more is required to support these kinds of objection, including justified principles that neither assume nor entertain facts of the sort a utilitarian considers. I know of no successful arguments like that: either comparable facts are assumed and entertained, or else appeal is made to strongly held but nevertheless corrigible moral convictions.

Perhaps one reason Dworkin does not think these cases can be distinguished on utilitarian grounds lies in the way he understands utilitarian arguments. He sees utilitarians as asking whether an admissions policy would satisfy the existing preferences of a given population. But that does not seem a reliable way to find out what a utilitarian wants to know—whether the policy would serve the interests of the population. One's interests are served by one's being placed in a position to get more of what one wants, that is, to get more satisfaction and less frustration, in the long run, and this cannot be guaranteed by simply following existing preferences. A white majority may strongly prefer racist policies, but there is good reason to believe that racist policies run counter to their interests in the long run (not to speak of the interests of the black minority). Despite their current preferences, they will be worse off under a racist system.

It may be objected that admissions officers do not decide what sort of system we shall all live under; they only decide one school's current policies. To discuss this adequately, I must dig deeper into some of Dworkin's general assumptions.

Dworkin writes as if every weight that could be placed upon the moral balance is either an argument based directly on a "reasonable policy goal" or else a right. This involves a very limited conception of moral deliberation, as well as of utilitarianism, and it may exaggerate the significance of his conclusions. Let us take the last point first.

Dworkin seeks a basis for distinguishing between racist and reverse discrimination and understands that his conclusions do not justify the latter. But he may still underestimate objections to reverse discrimination, for his model of moral reasoning ignores such factors as principles that may not be regarded as fundamental but are nevertheless believed to hold without exception. Such a principle could underlie objections to reverse discrimination.

The sort of principle I have in mind is illustrated in Mill's theory of liberty. Mill's conception of utility may be unorthodox since he places a premium upon "higher" pleasures (in *Utilitarianism)* and correspondingly upon the development in each individual of one's distinctively human capacities (in *On Liberty*). But it is clear that his basic principle is a form of utilitarianism and that he does not value liberty for its own sake. Nevertheless, he claims that "the only purpose for which power can rightfully be exercised over any member of any civilized community, against his will, is to prevent harm to others." Mill recognizes that he must argue substantively for this principle, even granted his utilitarianism; he must show, for example, that paternalistic legislation should never be entertained, though it is intended to help others and might sometimes actually serve the general welfare. Mill believes that, once we allow arguments besides "self-protection" to weigh in our deliberations about limitations on personal liberty, we are as a matter of fact bound to misuse our social power, to the detriment of the general welfare in the long run.

Mill believes that the general welfare will be served only if we *make it a matter of principle* never to use our power over others save for the purpose of preventing harm. The stakes are so high, he thinks, and the risks so great that a blanket prohibition is necessary and warranted. Mill may be wrong about the facts, but his position is intelligible. He sees the principle of liberty as derivative, not fundamental, and yet he lays it down as admitting no exceptions, given the facts as they are.

It would be possible for someone to reject reverse discrimination in a similar manner by endorsing a nondiscrimination principle. Indeed I think it likely that such reasoning underlies objections of some, at least, who also reject racism. They fully appreciate the moral difference between reverse and racist discrimination (as drawn by Dworkin, for example) and yet reject reverse discrimination thoroughly as counterproductive. They believe that racism can effectively be fought, in the long run, only by deliberately refusing to employ racial distinctions in these ways. Now, this approach to the elimination of racism may be mistaken; it may even be naive; and it needs in any case to be supported by some argument. But it is certainly intelligible, and so it cannot be ignored.

The possibility of reasoning with such a nondiscrimination principle underscores the point we have already made about Dworkin's conclusions. Since one can accept the distinction between *De Funis* and *Sweatt* while embracing such a principle, the distinction alone does not show that the two cases should be decided differently.

The possibility of reasoning with such a principle has wider implications. Its use cannot be understood as a direct case-by-case appeal to some "reasonable policy goal." Its point is rather that we should not be guided by the (real or imagined) effects of our particular decisions. In order to achieve certain goals, we must follow such a principle instead. And, if any such principle is at all tenable, it, too, cannot be outweighed by mere minimal or marginal utilities, not even when the general welfare is ultimately to be served, for it prescribes a long-term policy precisely in the face of such utilities.

Our original example illustrated how utility itself can argue for such principles. Mill's principle of liberty cannot, in his view, be overridden by utilities in particular cases. His idea would seem to be that policies soundly predicated on the general welfare, and designed to take precedence over ordinary appeals to utility, must be allowed to do so.

Thus Dworkin implies, at least by omission, too narrow a conception of the role played by utility in moral reasoning. In his article he fails to acknowledge such indirect utilitarian arguments. As a consequence, he also fails to note that utilitarians, such as Mill, have held that moral rights are ultimately grounded on considerations of utility, through the medium of moral rules.[4]

It may be noted that in "Taking Rights Seriously" Dworkin recognized the possibility of indirect utilitarian arguments, such as claims that the general welfare will best be served, in the long run, if we "treat violations of dignity and equality as special moral crimes, beyond the reach of ordinary moral justification."[5] Perhaps Dworkin does not note such possibilities in his present article because he thinks that all such arguments are groundless, or speculative at best. In any case, he said he did not know of any good arguments along these lines. Well, I am not sure that Mill's famous argument for the principle of liberty is quite what Dworkin had in mind, but it certainly indicates the possibility of indirect applications of utility; it places coercive social interference within a certain realm of human conduct "beyond the reach of ordinary utilitarian justification," as Dworkin requires, and I believe it cannot be dismissed out of hand.

Nor was Mill the first to advance arguments for the indirect application of fundamental values to conduct. A couple of examples should suffice. In the *Republic,* Plato tries to show the personal value of being a certain type of person who simply will not choose certain types of action. Plato can be understood as claiming that there are personal utilities attached to being a person, utilities that cannot be obtained in any other way, and which outweigh disadvantages in the long run. Plato may have been mistaken, but his position is intelligible.

Butler argued in this way more explicitly. His argument is, in fact, more useful to a utilitarian than to one concerned primarily with prudential considerations. He suggests (rather plausibly, I think) that we would all be better off if we had more sympathetic concern for other people. This has implications for action since we can affect our own attitudes and—most important—what sort of people our children will be.

The utilitarian version of Butler's argument has further bearing on Dworkin's treatment of utilitarianism. Dworkin wishes utilitarians to discount certain types of preference in order to avoid a clash between its calculations and the right to equal consideration.

But a utilitarian might well argue on *utilitarian* grounds that we should make it a matter of principle to discount such attitudes, because that is required if we are to serve the general welfare in the long run. Some of the attitudes that worry Dworkin are good examples. Experience shows, I believe, not only that racist practices are contrary to the general welfare but also that the corresponding attitudes (on which the practices are often blamed) are both reinforced by those practices and extinguished by their elimination. These attitudes should not be taken for granted. For such reasons, we should not simply be guided by existing preferences. Greater benefits, less suffering and hardship, can be reaped in the long run if we try to change them.

Dworkin says we must discount altruistic preferences too, but he seems to be thinking only of those that favor certain classes of persons. In any case, the ones that would be favored by a utilitarian are those that serve the general welfare in the long run. If the stakes are high enough, and such attitudes as generalized benevolence can be effectively "reinforced," a utilitarian may wish us systematically to give them extra weight in our deliberations, just as he may wish us to discount attitudes that are both counterproductive and "extinguishable."

I can say something in reply to the objection that because admissions officers do not decide what sort of social system we shall live under, they cannot be affected by all these considerations; their decisions are much more limited. It may be said that a utilitarian must forsake the "classical" position of unqualified commitment to the general welfare if he wishes to be guided by these considerations, since isolated actions on such policies are likely not to serve the general welfare but to be self-defeating. Only rule-utilitarians are willing to commit themselves to "ideal" utilitarian policies when action in accordance with them will not serve the general welfare.

I shall offer just two comments here. The circumstances in which it becomes reasonable, from a utilitarian point of view, to act upon such policies are not easy to determine. But it does not follow that it is never reasonable for a utilitarian to act upon such policies. In the. first place, the decisions of officials, as opposed to private individuals, have relatively large-scale effects: the public arena—with which we are here concerned—is most likely to provide suitable conditions.

In the second place, a utilitarian might reason as follows. Suppose I do not know what to do because my decision literally depends on what others, in similar circumstances, will decide to do; but their position is similar to mine in this very respect too. Others' decisions simply cannot be taken as given. Suppose, further, that if everyone in a position like mine followed an ideal policy, the results would be far better than if we all were guided by the direct advantages and disadvantages of our isolated decisions. What it is best for me to do in any situation must be what it is best for anyone to do in a similar position. It follows that the best thing, from a utilitarian point of view, for each of us to do must be to follow the ideal policy. In circumstances such as these, for example, in the private as well as in the public arena, one can sometimes argue soundly for adherence to an ideal policy, contrary to existing preferences.

Finally, utilitarians will no doubt reject Dworkin's suggestion that they revise their theory. The difficulty he wishes to avoid for them is a conflict between the right to equal consideration and the unrestricted counting of external preferences. Dworkin supposes that most utilitarian sympathizers hold more fundamentally to the right and so should willingly adjust utilitarian calculations to accommodate it. But utilitarians will undoubtedly protest that, if there is any such right, it must be grounded in (not assumed by) utility. Dworkin simply does not entertain such possibilities.

But even if we supposed there was such a right, I am uncertain how to decide whether it does in fact conflict with external preferences. Dworkin suggests unclear tests, and a variety of them; he speaks of "treatment as an equal," "equal respect," and "equal concern," for example. But what do these amount to? How do we decide when one fails to give equal respect or equal concern? Dworkin is quite clear that unequal treatment is no criterion, for that is compatible with equal consideration—as when I give more medicine to the sicker person. But this means that certain differences between individuals and their circumstances warrant different treatments, without denying equal consideration. If differences of need are relevant, why not differences in merit or desert? Why should we assume, for example, that an aristocrat, who believes that members of the lower social orders ought to get smaller shares of wealth and income, does not give them equal consideration? Why is his attitude toward them relevantly different from the attitude that Dworkin approves toward one who needs less medicine than others? Until we are able to answer these questions, we cannot know why there is a relevant difference between the need for an extremely expensive dialysis machine, for example, and the "external preference" that those who need dialysis machines should get them, even at great cost.

A troublesome aspect of Dworkin's article is the elusive character of the right to treatment as an equal. I am uncertain what it is a right to, how one respects or violates it. And I believe the root of this difficulty is the lack of an argument for it. If we had some idea of how it was supposed to be grounded, we would have an idea of how it is to be defined.

### Notes

1. Emphasis added.
2. *New York Review of Books,* December 17, 1970, reprinted in *Oxford Essays in Jurisprudence,* 2d series, ed. A. W. B. Simpson (Oxford: The Clarendon Press, 1973). The quotation is from p. 211 in Simpson.
3. *Oxford Essays,* p. 211.
4. I have discussed this further in "Mill's Theory of Morality," *Nous* 10 (1976): 101-120 and in "Human Rights and the General Welfare," *Philosophy and Public Affairs* 6 (1977): 113-129.
5. *Oxford Essays,* p. 220, n. 4.

# 7

# Reverse discrimination reversed

**MARK R. MacGUIGAN**

Professor Dworkin has done us a signal service by introducing, I believe for the first time in Canada in a sustained intellectual way, a debate that has heretofore been dramatically staged in the journals, forums, and courts in the United States. The subject of reverse discrimination will be as much a part of our future as of that of the United States, for it is already, largely unnoticed, a part of our present.

The requirement of veterans' preferences by the law covering public service hiring has not excited much opposition over the years, but not so the introductory statement by the Public Service Commission of Canada in its *Annual Report, 1971:*

> The question we have been asking ourselves recently is this: Is a public service that does not fully represent the people it serves the best possible public service? And if not, how can we ensure that there is true equality of opportunity for all peoples when it comes to being considered for appointment or promotion in the public service?
>
> The answer may be found in a dynamic concept of merit, one which is able to adapt to the real conditions and the changing values of society at large. It is this philosophy that lies behind the recent introduction of special recruitment programs for French-speaking Canadians, of programs aimed at improving the opportunities for female public servants, and our newly-launched Native employment program. It is a preoccupation we will be increasingly facing in the future.[1]

A storm burst almost immediately. The most trenchant critic was probably Senator Eugene Forsey:

> Honourable senators, this is plain nonsense from start to finish. It is pure Humpty Dumptyism. "When I use a word," said Humpty Dumpty, "it

means just what I choose it to mean." Spreading the opportunity to compete, or "equal access" may be a good principle; but it is no more an "element" of the merit principle than soup is an "element" of fish. The "equal access" principle is not only not "closely related" to the merit principle: it is totally unrelated, and may be in direct and flagrant conflict with it. . . .

Now, of course, a civil service made up exclusively of people from one area of the country, one ethnic or religious group, one province, one region, one age, one sex, would be highly undesirable and, I may add, highly unlikely. It wouldn't be ideal, it wouldn't be desirable and it is not likely to happen and it is daily becoming less likely. But it does not follow that we should scrap the merit system for a quota system. We do not have to see a situation where a highly qualified applicant for a position in the public service is told, "Sorry: the Nova Scotia quota (or the Alberta quota, or the Eskimo quota, or whatever it may be) is full." Nor, of course, does the commission's report suggest quite that. It does seem to hint that the merit system should be modified by a hemi-demi-semi quota system; that it should be a merit system with knobs on, or holes in it.[2]

Whatever may have been the intentions of the Public Service Commission, the Government clarified the most sensitive question, that of language, in a resolution Parliament passed in 1973. Prime Minister Pierre Trudeau spelled out the practical consequences for the English-speaking majority this way:

Today's resolution is quite specific. It states that unilingual public servants will be given at least one year's notice of the bilingual designation of their posts. They will have an opportunity to take language training—also at public expense—or to transfer to a unilingual position at no loss of salary.

What if someone should decline language training or be unsuccessful at it, and also refuse a transfer? If all that befalls him, he may remain in his post if he wishes to and we will make administrative arrangements to ensure that the bilingual needs of his office are met. In other words, no public servant will be removed from his position by virtue of our implementation of the principles.[3]

The success of the public service programs in promoting the employment of minority groups is open to question. The Public Service Commission's 1973 *Annual Report,* released in September 1974, claims that the commission's determination to make the federal public service bilingual is succeeding. However, with respect to the advancement of women to government executive positions, the conclusion of a recent newspaper analysis is that "women are unequal in the federal public service and appear to be losing ground despite trumpeted campaigns aimed at the recruitment, training and promotion of qualified women."[4]

The question of reverse discrimination was also raised by the *Statement of the Government of Canada on Indian Policy, 1969:*

> The Government believes that its policies must lead to the full, free and non-discriminatory participation of the Indian people in Canadian society. Such a goal requires a break with the past. It requires that the Indian people's role of dependence be replaced by a role of *equal status,* opportunity and responsibility, a role they can share with all other Canadians.[5]

And again: "To be an Indian must be to be free—free to develop Indian cultures in an environment of *legal, social and economic equality* with other Canadians."[6] The problem was that the promise of equality spelled the end of the special status that Indians had and wanted more fully. They were quick to reply, with a phrase from the Hawthorn Report of 1967 *(A Survey of the Contemporary Indians of Canada),* that they must be regarded as "citizens plus." A presentation bearing this name, made to the Prime Minister in June 1970 by the Indian chiefs of Alberta, argued that "equality in law precludes discrimination of any kind; whereas equality in fact may involve the necessity of different treatment in order to obtain a result which establishes an equilibrium between different situations."[7]

While positive discrimination in favor of Indians was being urged, negative discrimination against them was being struck down by the Canadian courts. In *Drybones,* in the first clear assertion of the supremacy of the 1960 Bill of Rights over other legislation, the Supreme Court of Canada struck down a section of the Indian Act that made it an offense for an Indian to be intoxicated off a reserve because it denied Indian equality before the law.[8] As Hall, J., put it in a concurring judgment:

> The Canadian Bill of Rights is not fulfilled if it merely equates Indians with Indians in terms of equality before the law, but can have validity and

meaning only when . . . it is seen to repudiate discrimination . . . by reason of race . . . in whatever way that discrimination may manifest itself not only as between Indian and Indian but as between all Canadians whether Indian or non-Indian.[9]

Unfortunately, in the subsequent *Lavell* case, which concerned sex rather than race discrimination, the same court failed to follow *Drybones*.[10] By a five to four margin, it held that "equality before the law" meant only in the administration or application of the law by the law enforcement authorities and the ordinary courts and that there was no such inequality of treatment where the Indian Act provided that the registrar delete from the Indian registry the names of Indian women (but not of Indian men) who married non-Indians. In a powerful dissent, Laskin, J. (as he then was), wrote:

> The gist of the judgment [in *Drybones*] lay in the legal disability imposed upon a person by reason of his race when other persons were under no similar restraint. If for the words "on account of race" there are substituted the words "on account of sex" the result must surely be the same where a federal enactment imposes disabilities or prescribed qualifications for members of the female sex which are not imposed upon the members of the male sex in the same circumstances.
>
> It is said, however, that although this may be so as between males and females in general, it does not follow where the distinction on the basis of sex is limited as here to members of the Indian race. . . .
>
> It appears to me that [this] contention . . . is one that compounds racial inequality even beyond the point that the *Drybones* case found unacceptable.[11]

The argument was squarely made in *Lavell* that the legislative scheme was a positive discrimination for the benefit of the Indian race. To quote again from Laskin, J.:

> It was urged, in reliance in part on history, that the discrimination embodied in the Indian Act under s. 12(1) (b) is based upon a reasonable classification of Indians as a race, that the Indian Act reflects this classification and that the paramount purpose of the Act to preserve and protect the members of the race is prevented by the statutory preference for Indian men. . . . I doubt whether discrimination on account of sex, where as here it has no biological or physiological rationale, could be sustained as a reasonable classification even if the direction against it was not as explicit as it is in the *Canadian Bill of Rights*.[12]

For Laskin, J., the result was a fortiori in the light of the Bill of Rights.

Turning now from the relevance to the content of Professor Dworkin's address, I should frankly admit at once that I cannot agree with his principal thesis, though I do accept the greater part of his analysis of the problem. I can agree with his initial principles that a policy of reverse discrimination may serve proper social goals like collective welfare and equality and that the state may not serve social goals at the expense of human rights. In fact, I would proclaim this latter as a fundamental principle, provided that human rights are not confused with property rights. In my view the state's power must be narrowly exercised toward nonmaterial freedoms and broadly exercised toward material freedoms.

I would also adopt Professor Dworkin's position that racial discrimination is bad when it infringes the right to treatment as equals but not when it violates the right to equal treatment. Justice requires not an equal quantity in the result but equal consideration in the decision.

But what does equal consideration mean for Professor Dworkin? If he were to mean only that whatever the rule for selecting candidates, those who apply it have to hew to standards of equal accuracy and equal individual consideration, then in practice a DeFunis has only the right to dispute whether he is in fact white and whether the techniques the school used to determine his color were tests of adequate accuracy. He could not ask whether there should be separate treatment for white and black, since that has already been decided beyond question by the initial classification. I would recall Canada's Mr. Justice Hall's words that it is not enough for equality merely to equate Indian with Indian. An arbitrary classification does not satisfy justice.[13]

Has Professor Dworkin made clear how one moves from equal protection, treatment, and consideration under given rules, whatever they may be, to equal protection, treatment, and consideration in deciding what the rules shall be? There can be no lighter standards for the latter than the former, yet the idea of equality is not the same in the two cases. But where I believe Dworkin goes seriously astray is in thinking that discrimination may ever be made on the basis of race. Granted, the individual does not have a right to an educational place as such. What he has is a right not to be discriminated against on the basis of race in competing for a place. In the words of Douglas, J., in *DeFunis,* "the consideration of race as a measure of an applicant's qualification normally introduces a capricious and irrelevant factor working an invidious discrimination."[14]

I have used the word "race," but I use it as shorthand for all the basic human groups—sex, color, religion, national origin, language. In fact, much of the debate has occurred with regard to discrimination based on sex. Judith Jarvis Thomson has defended a policy of preferential hiring for blacks and women jointly over white males as a form of compensation for the wrongs they have suffered, and she does not shrink from the consequences:

> Of course choosing this way of making amends means that the costs are imposed on the young white male applicants who are turned away. And so it should be noticed that it is not entirely inappropriate that these applicants should pay the costs. No doubt few, if any, have themselves, individually, done any wrongs to blacks and women. But they have profited from the wrongs the community did. Many may actually have been direct beneficiaries of policies which excluded or downgraded blacks and women— perhaps in school admissions, perhaps in access to financial aid, perhaps elsewhere; and even those who did not directly benefit in this way had, at any rate, the advantage in the competition which comes of confidence in one's full membership, and of one's rights being recognized as a matter of course.[15]

Professor Dworkin might not share these sentiments, but I believe his position leads to the same result: the sacrifice of the equal opportunity of the individual members of the majority group.

To state my own position, I would distinguish between direct loss to individuals and a general social loss in which they would share with everyone else. In my view racial discrimination in setting standards is never justifiable where it causes direct loss to individuals, as in the case of jobs and university places. It may be justifiable, however, where it involves giving additional benefits to members of minority groups without any direct loss to individuals in the majority group. In such a case the burden is borne by the whole community and not by a small number of individuals. The cost is borne generally by the majority group and not by individual members of the majority group. Reverse discrimination is thus permissible only when it is positive in effect and does not transgress individual rights—in other words, when it is reverse discrimination reversed so that it benefits all of society.

This view would still allow the remedying of the consequences of discrimination against minority groups by unusual or special consideration for members of these groups. Although I believe that absolute quotas and preferences are absolutely wrong, there is nothing wrong about numerical targets, provided that they remain tentative and yield when necessary to the prior claim of equality of individual consideration. The absence of opportunity of a particular group, as measured by its absence of achievement, does not justify a quota, but it is highly relevant evidence that the traditional standards discriminate against that group. Every form of encouragement and assistance may then be given to members of that group short of a bar to members of another group.

I am happy to adopt the eloquent prose of Douglas, J.:

The Equal Protection Clause did not enact a requirement that Law Schools employ as the sole criterion for admissions a formula based upon the LSAT and undergraduate grades, nor does it proscribe law schools from evaluating an applicant's prior achievements in light of the barriers that he had to overcome. A Black applicant who pulled himself out of the ghetto into a junior college may thereby demonstrate a level of motivation, perseverance and ability that would lead a fairminded admissions committee to conclude that he shows more promise for law study than the son of a rich alumnus who achieved better grades at Harvard. That applicant would not be offered admission because he is Black, but because as an individual he has shown he has the potential, while the Harvard man may have taken less advantage of the vastly superior opportunities offered him. Because of the weight of the prior handicaps, that Black applicant may not realize his full potential in the first year of law school, or even in the full three years, but in the long pull of a legal career his achievements may far outstrip those of his classmates whose earlier records appeared superior by conventional criteria. There is currently no test available to the admissions committee that can predict such possibilities with assurance, but the committee may nevertheless seek to gauge it as best as it can, and weight this factor in its decisions. Such a policy would not be limited to Blacks, or Chicanos or Filipinos or American Indians, although undoubtedly groups such as these may in practice be the principal beneficiaries of it. But a poor Appala-chian white, or a second generation Chinese in San Francisco, or some other American whose lineage is so diverse as to defy ethnic labels, may demonstrate similar potential and thus be accorded favorable considera-tion by the committee.

The difference between such a policy and the one presented by this case is that the committee would be making decisions on the basis of individual attributes, rather than according a preference solely on the basis of race.[16]

I do not want to be misunderstood as only grudgingly accepting the necessity of compensatory justice for minorities. My obliga-tions as a commentator have limited the orientation of my remarks, but I would unqualifiedly endorse the recognition of factual as well as legal equality as the prime goal of political action through the state. In particular, compensatory legislation, compensatory stan-dards, and compensatory administration are in my opinion among the most important needs today. As a general statement of my political philosophy, provided that it was heard with the qualifica-tions I have already expressed, I could want nothing better than the refrain of the late President Magsaysay of the Philippines: "I be-lieve that he who has less in life should have more in law."

What we are talking about is not the direction but the pace of social change. I think we are all agreed, in a liberal democracy, on helping the hindmost. We must not allow ourselves to fear the pace itself of the social changes that must be effected to achieve equality. But we must refrain from solving injustice by creating injustice, even if we regard the new injustices as puny in comparison with the old ones. If started they will breed their own train of followers, not the least of which are the evils of envy and resentment. Let us not be afraid to work and to wait for success. The mills of justice grind slowly, but they grind exceeding fine.

### Notes

1. Public Service Commission of Canada, *Annual Report* (1971), p. 1.
2. Canada, Senate, *Debates,* June 14, 1972, p. 481.
3. Canada, Commons, *Debates,* May 31, 1973, p. 4305.
4. *Toronto Globe and Mail,* Oct. 18, 1974, p. 8.

5. *Statement of the Government of Canada on Indian Policy* (1969), p. 5. (Emphasis added.)
6. Ibid., p. 3. (Emphasis added.)
7. "Citizens Plus," unpublished material by the Alberta Chiefs, 1970, p. 5.
8. (1970) S.C.R. 282.
9. Ibid., p. 300.
10. (1970) 38 D.L.R. (3d) 481.
11. Ibid., pp. 507-508.
12. Ibid., p. 510.
13. Editor's note: In the revised version of "DeFunis and Sweatt" above, Professor Dworkin became responsive to this criticism; Dr. MacGuigan had said that Dworkin was not so responsive in the original paper, "Freedom and Dignity in the Law," delivered at the colloquium. MacGuigan's former comments have been revised in this paragraph and the next.
14. 94 S.Ct. 1704, at 1714 (1974).
15. J. J. Thomson, "Preferential Hiring," *Philosophy and Public Affairs* 2 (1973): 383-384.
16. *DeFunis v. Odegaard,* 94 S.Ct. 1704, at 1713 (1974).

# Part III.   ADJUDICATION

# 8

# Introduction

## RICHARD BRONAUGH

One may go to court on a matter of one's own business or be hauled in upon a matter of public concern. But whether one is suing some other person for a civil wrong or has been charged with a criminal offense, going to court is a way of entering a contest. In civil private legal matters, it is a contest that never need be entered; one may choose not to sue. And if one is threatened with a suit, one may choose to settle out of court. A plea of guilty or no-contest normally will resolve the question of criminal wrongdoing. On the other hand, for those who choose to play, the purpose is immanent in the contest; it is dispute settlement.

The rules and broad patterns of the possible kinds of contest vary; the particular sort examined by the three writers here is an adversarial adjudication. The most important characteristic of any adjudicative procedure—whether adversarial or otherwise—is that it attempts, through the office of a third party, to reach a decision controlled largely by the merits of the case. An adjudication is not the only way. The disputants could be locked in a room until they reached agreement. But this method is the same as lacking a legal procedure. Why should anyone turn up at court to be placed in a room with someone with whom he has so far been unable to settle in the space of all outdoors? (If the room were lined with books of law, at least they would have heavy things to throw at each other. That would be a method of combat.) Factors extrinsic to the situation could be used to decide the dispute—for example, a throw of a fair die, appeal to an oracle, the throw of a crooked die, the strength of a family or political connection, the best guess of the cat's next cough, medieval ordeals. In the Middle Ages it was God's job to decide issues, which Thompson and Johnson describe in *An Introduction to Medieval Europe, 300-1500:*

One of the commonest methods of appeal to God was compurgation, which gave the defendant a decided advantage. The accused swore to the truth of his story, usually on relics of the saints, and brought forth a group of oath-helpers, or compurgators, to swear that in their opinion his oath was good. Originally the compurgators were members of the family, then simply neighbors or other persons; their number varied according to the importance of the charge and the accused person. The Merovingian Queen Fredegund used three bishops and three hundred nobles as compurgators to establish the paternity of her child. The theory of compurgation, of course, was that God would punish the perjurer, as indeed the state did if the compurgator were found to be lying. But it proved to be too easy a way to escape punishment, and lost favor when the study of Roman law was revived in the twelfth century.

The person chosen to undergo the ordeal of hot water was obliged to retrieve some small object from a kettle of boiling water. If after a short period, usually three days, his hand and arm were found to be healing properly, God had established the truth of his assertions. Obviously the case was actually decided by the persons who determined whether God had caused the injury to heal properly or not. In some cases there was no need to wait. Gregory of Tours reports that in a dispute between an orthodox Christian believer and an Arian heretic, when resort was had to the ordeal of hot water, an orthodox deacon reached into the boiling pot and drew out a ring and "suffered no harm, protesting rather that at the bottom the kettle was cold while at the top it was pleasantly warm." The Arian was emboldened in like manner to establish his innocence, but "as soon as his hand had been thrust in, all the flesh was boiled off the bones clear up to the elbow." In the ordeal of cold water the person under examination was thrown bound into some body of water. "And ... whoever after the invocation of God ... seeks to hide the truth by a lie, cannot be submerged in the water above which the voice of the Lord God had thundered; for the pure nature of the water recognizes as impure, and therefore rejects as inconsistent with itself, such human nature as has once been regenerated by the waters of baptism and is again infected by falsehood." Other ordeals were the red-hot iron, the glowing plowshares, and the fire, and there were still others. In the ordeal of the cross both contestants held their arms straight out from their sides, and God justified him who held out his arms the longer time. Trial by battle was perhaps the most popular of all the ordeals; like the ordeal of the cross it required the participation of both plaintiff and defendant, and it furnished spectators the best show. Women and clergy were represented by champions.

Adjudication, the method of law, can be done in various ways;

the adversary system—which is said to derive from the method of combat—is only one of them. In addition there are the inquisition, or the method of holding an inquest or inquiry; the method of conference, in which, as in civil actions in Germany, the parties meet with a third party, a judge who works out a solution in accordance with supposedly fixed legal rules; and mediation, in which a third party attempts to develop some compromise through appeals to the interests of the disputants (this system is not truly *adjudicative,* yet resembles it in practice when rights are claimed). In any system of adjudication the third party could take several forms as well. There might be a body of jurists or a mix of professionals and non-professionals at law or a jury of one's peers or a single trained (French) civil servant.

Given these possibilities, how can one discuss justice in dispute settlement without a comparison of all these methods? Even if one excludes combat and the extrinsic methods, is it not necessary at least to compare several systems of adjudication? Fascinating as it would be, it is the presupposition of the approach of the following three writers that it is not necessary to do so. In fact, it may be more difficult than it looks even to attempt such a comparison. Consider the sense of the following demonstration: Conferences in Germany yield justice 90 percent of the time, whereas justice is achieved in England only 80 percent of the time under the adversarial approach. Therefore England could improve its record by going to the conference method. That is a non sequitur, even if the conclusion were true. Different systems may be suited to different peoples. (It is not certain that Canadians will score more goals if they try to play hockey as the Russians do.) These methods are only a matter of emphasis and idealization anyway; adjudication and mediation can touch, and the pretrial conference in U.S. civil litigation is a tendency away from courtroom battle toward the German system. Yet there is perhaps less faith in authority in North America than in Germany, and so the adversarial finale may continue to be sought as necessary to give people the sense that law, not man, settled the dispute in their case.

# 9

# On the adversary system and justice

MARTIN P. GOLDING

From the traditional view, the trial, civil or criminal, is a process for answering disputed questions of fact, attendant to which the case is decided by applying appropriate rules of law to the facts as determined. In Anglo-American jurisdictions the characteristic procedure (with perhaps a few exceptions) for answering such questions is adversarial in form. This appears true as a matter of law as well as general practice. As Justice Jackson stated in *Hickman* v. *Taylor* (329 U.S. 495, 516), "A common law trial is and always should be an adversary proceeding." Indeed the adversary system is often vaunted as one of the excellences of the Anglo-American law and, moreover, as a method of justice no better than which can be conceived.

The adversary system, just as any other feature of the law, can be discussed from a variety of perspectives. It has, for example, recently become the subject of lively debate in the public press, as well as within the confines of the law guild itself, as an important part of the larger issue of the social responsibilities of the lawyer. In this essay I want to examine the adversary system in so far as it plays a central role in the courthouse way of settling disputes. In particular, I propose to examine the principal justifications that have been given for the adversary system and to evaluate its status as a method of justice. We shall find that each of the justifications seems to rely on a particular conception of justice or, more accurately, some facet of the concept of justice. I shall, however, not attempt to determine whether these conceptions are expressions of some single principle of justice; but I do want to consider the bearing of the idea of procedural fairness on the various justifications. My discussion, I believe, is of great relevance to the problems of professional ethics to which the adversary system gives rise, but I shall deal with them only very tangentially. (The area of dispute settlement, of which my immediate subject is only a small part, has been relatively neglected by moral philosophers, and I hope that this essay, whatever its merits, at least serves to stimulate interest in this rich territory.)

I shall begin by analyzing the concept of a trial in order to fix its position within the area of dispute settlement. This will provide a context for the next section, which is devoted to the justifications of the adversary system. It is important to recognize that trials at law constitute only a small, though significant, portion of the field of justice and of the just ordering of relations between individuals and between individuals and the state. It is also important to see that an adversary type of proceeding is not the only form that a trial might take. What, then, is a trial?[1]

I think that there is hardly anything novel in adopting a dispute settlement approach to this question. It is in fact almost standard in legal circles to view the trial process as a kind of dispute settling. Thus it was trials that the late Karl N. Llewellyn had in mind when he said that the primary purpose of law is to "settle disputes which do not otherwise get settled."[2] Although this statement in my opinion grossly exaggerates the role of trials in the larger picture of the law, it nevertheless provides a useful starting point for an analysis of the concept. Llewellyn's statement contains the helpful suggestion that a trial at law is a second-level process for achieving a dispute settlement that was not achieved at the first level. This process is, of course, much more than just another round of talks between parties to a conflict, for there is present at the trial something that was absent from the earlier attempts at settlement.

This new factor consists in the introduction of a third party (an outsider, a person or group that is not party to the dispute) into the conflict situation. In order to understand the distinctive office of the third party in the trial process, it is useful to compare different types of third-party dispute settlement; for just as a trial is a special kind of dispute settling in that it involves a third party, it is also a special kind of a third-party dispute settling. Third parties may in fact play a variety of roles in the resolution of conflict.

This point is frequently exemplified in everyday life. For instance, when two neighbors have a spat over such humdrum matters as putting out the trash or playing a musical instrument late at night, a third neighbor might step in and help them settle their differences. He might do this in a number of ways: he might give each party a better understanding of the needs of the other, or make a fresh suggestion, and thereby assist them in reaching a compromise; or he might simply soothe ruffled feelings by getting them to discuss the problem. Such everyday occurrences have analogues in specialized fields of dispute settlement (such as labor mediation, marriage counseling, or family therapy). The friendly neighbor might also be called on by the parties to settle their dispute by *adjudicating* their controversy—that is, by making a decision as to who is in the right and who is in the wrong, who wins and who loses. In this case his activity would parallel that of the judge, or of the judge and jury, in the trial at law.

This last comparison, however, is only rough because, in addition to a trial, there are other modes of adjudication that are specialized counterparts of the neighbor's activity. Just as we must differentiate adjudication from mediation and family therapy—which do not easily lend themselves to winner-loser terminology—so must we also distinguish the trial from two other modes of adjudication. The first of these is that mode in which the third party has expert knowledge of the subject matter of the controversy and is called upon to decide a dispute by applying this expert knowledge rather than general rules of law. This circumstance frequently obtains in the field of commercial arbitration. The garment manufacturing industry provides plentiful examples. Although speed and low cost are undoubtedly major considerations in resorting to arbitration rather than litigation in the courts, the expertise of the arbitrator is also frequently a factor. For instance, when there is disagreement between a manufacturer and a supplier on whether the quality of the goods delivered is of the quality of the goods ordered, the issue will be put to an impartial person with experience in the field.

In the trial situation, on the other hand, characteristically the third party is not required to have expert knowledge of the subject under dispute. In jury trials, in fact, the possession of expert knowledge may be used as grounds for excluding a prospective juror from sitting on a case. It is, of course, occasionally true that because of the complexity of the subject matter, a special master may be appointed to hear a dispute. If this procedure were generally adopted, it would constitute a fundamental reform of our method of trial adjudication. It might also be added that the Anglo-American judge does not have in hand anything like the investigative file (dossier) supplied to the continental judge before the hearing of a case. This is not to say that the trial judge begins in a state of total ignorance; there are pleadings and pretrial proceedings. But the information he possesses comes to him from the partisan adversaries, not from an independent investigating judicial officer.

Second, a trial should be distinguished from adjudication in which disputes are decided by applying rules, but rules that are the creatures of the private agreement of the parties. This situation obtains, for example, in grievance arbitration under a labor management contract. Though an arbitrator's award may be legally binding and enforceable in the courts, the rules that he applies have been privately negotiated between the parties. In a trial, however, the rules in point are those of the public legal system; furthermore, the decision is rendered by a public official (a judge) or by individuals (a jury) acting for the community. The public nature of the rules and the public office of the third party have a bearing on the justifications of the adversary system. (Nonpublic adjudication, which I am not considering here, requires a slightly different treatment.)

Let me summarize my attempt to clarify the concept of a trial as a special type of third-party dispute settlement. This clarification has proceeded by distinguishing third-party dispute settling from bilateral negotiation, by distinguishing adjudication from other kinds of third-party dispute settling, and by distinguishing trials from other modes of adjudication. The similarities and differences among these forms of dispute settlement raise the problem of the extent to which standards of procedural fairness are invariant, that is, whether the same standards of fairness are applicable to the various kinds of dispute settlement. I shall not be concerned with this problem here, but I shall later want to consider some aspects of procedural fairness in relation to the adversary system.[3] Thus a trial has the following significant features. (1) It consists in the settlement of a dispute by a third party who is not necessarily an expert on the matter under dispute. (2) The settlement is effected by the rendering of a decision made in accordance with rules. (3) The rules in question are rules of the public legal system. To this list a fourth item should be added, which is actually implicit in the previous account but which deserves to be emphasized because it will be important in my subsequent discussion. (4) The decision that effects the settlement is intended as a final resolution of the controversy. This feature is one that trials share with other modes of adjudication. In a moment I shall say more about this fourth item. Before I do that, I feel it urgent to qualify one aspect of the dispute-settlement approach.

I began my discussion of the concept of a trial by following up a suggestion given by Llewellyn's view that the primary purpose of law is "to settle disputes which do not otherwise get settled." It seems to me that Llewellyn's expression is in fact highly misleading in regard to a large and important category of trials: criminal trials. The notion that trials settle disputes that do not otherwise get settled is appropriate to civil litigation but not to the criminal trial. It is true that in both the civil and criminal contexts lawyers function as agent-negotiators and fixers, and a defense attorney might plea bargain and sentence bargain for his client. But it is fundamentally misleading to think of a criminal trial as a second-level process that is initiated when the bargaining stage results in failure—and all the more so if the client proclaims his innocence from the start. It is important to mention this qualification because most of the recent controversy over the adversary system has concerned the criminal trial.

Nevertheless, this qualification in no way negatives the conclusions we have reached on the features of the trial. In logical terms a criminal trial is just as much, and in precisely the same sense, a contentious affair (a dispute, a controversy) as a civil suit. The characteristics attributed to the trial apply to both its civil and criminal varieties; thus a criminal trial can be legitimately called the settling of a dispute by the rendering of a decision. The criminal and civil trial have in common certain essential logical features.

To amplify this point, let me turn back to the fourth item mentioned above: the decision, which is intended as a final resolution of the controversy. This is the aim, the end, of the trial process. But what about its beginning, its initiation? If a decision in the case is

supposed to bring the trial to a close, are there no logical preconditions that make this kind of closure possible? There in fact seem
to be at least two preconditions of this sort, and in order to explain
them it will be useful to take another look at third-party dispute
settling of the noncriminal variety. As before, my conclusions will
also be applicable to the criminal trial. What, then, are the preconditions of "finality"?

A slight shift in the dispute-settling perspective supplies a clue.
Instead of thinking of the trial at law as a second-level process that
follows upon the failure of a first-level process of dispute settlement, let us view the trial as a second-level process that follows
upon conflict at a prior level. Putting the matter in this way enables
us to see that a trial does not necessarily resolve the conflict of the
prior level. All depends on what we mean by the settlement of a dispute and on the relationship that the dispute at the second level is
supposed to have to the original conflict. Thus, in the case of litigation between members of a family, the conflict may actually be ex-
acerbated even though their dispute is settled at the second level.
Plainly, a given conflict may have emotional overtones that are in no
way allayed by the third party's decision. But it is not merely the
possible presence of emotional factors that makes it a mistake to
think that the prior conflict is necessarily resolved by a decision at
the second level. Underlying any conflict there often is a complex of
opposed interests, values, wants, needs, personality structures,
styles of life, and so forth that may to a great extent remain in a
state of opposition long after the decision in a case is rendered at
the second level. A trial at law appears to be ill suited for the resolution of certain types of conflict; and in order to resolve the full-
blown original conflict, such nonadjudicatory processes as concili-
ation and therapeutic integration may have to be called into service.

If all this is the case, how can a decision by a third party ever be
the final resolution of a dispute? What are the logical preconditions
of finality? The first point to be noticed is that the dispute that is
settled by the third party is not the original conflict, with all its overtones and complexities, but rather the controversy that is presented by the parties for resolution. In order to achieve finality in
the adjudicatory situation, the original conflict is superseded by the
second-level dispute that is presented to the third party. Moreover,

the second-level controversy has to be presented in a certain form: the matter at issue in the second-level dispute must be delimited and given a relatively precise formulation in a proposition or set of propositions. Second, the proposition must be one over which the parties disagree in a logical sense. Thus, the rivalry between King Francis and the Emperor Charles, in which Francis asserted "was mein Bruder Karl haben will [the city of Milan], das will ich auch haben," was a genuine conflict; but there was no logical opposition between the desire that each had for the city of Milan. In our case, however, what is required is a proposition that is asserted by the one party and denied by the other. In a trial at law, the matter at issue is usually expressed in terms of one party's claim of a right or entitlement that is rejected by the other party, but this may be more a requirement of legal technique than anything else.

In sum, then, the proposition (or set of propositions) that is being asserted by one side and denied by the other and, therefore, the proposition that has to be decided on by the third party, has to be fairly clear. In this way definition is achieved for the ambit of the dispute, that is, for the subordinate propositions that have to be established in order to reach a decision on the controverted proposition. Rules of pleading delimit and give a relatively precise definition to the controversy and secure "joinder of issue"—logical opposition between the parties. Unless the disputed issue is given a relatively precise formulation in propositional terms, it will hardly be clear whether the decision rendered does in fact resolve the controversy with finality.

With this statement of two of the logical preconditions of the trial process, I have completed the first part of my program. (There is a third precondition, though the two mentioned are enough for our purposes: the relief being requested must be something that is feasible for the dispute settler to award.) We have until now concentrated on the trial's beginning (its logical preconditions) and its end (the decision, made in accordance with public rules of law, which resolves the dispute with finality). It is now time to focus upon the middle of the trial process, the part that most people would rightly regard as its heart. This is the hearing stage of the trial, when argument and evidence are obtained by the third party (the court, as we can now simply call it) on the subordinate propositions that have to be established in order to render a decision on the controverted issue. These propositions are just as much in contention as the controverted issue. These are the disputed questions of fact that I referred to when I characterized the trial earlier.

Our present problem is, Why adopt the adversary system as the method for determining answers to those disputed questions of fact on which the ultimate decision in a case depends? The investigation of the concept of a trial has revealed the precise sense in which a trial is a dispute, a controversial affair. This specifically controversial character of trials is in no way altered by whether they are adversarial trials or instead follow some other system of procedure (such as judicial investigation or judicial prosecution). There seems to be nothing in the nature of trials that would necessitate employment of the adversary system. Its justification is still open. This problem is the second part of my program, which I shall begin with a brief account of what the adversary system is.

This system (or method) has been well described by Professor Lon L. Fuller as a "philosophy of adjudication." It is a philosophy that insists on keeping distinct the function of the advocate from that of the judge, or of the judge from that of the jury; the decision of the case is for the judge, or for the judge and jury. That decision must be as objective and as free from bias as it possibly can, and judgment must be withheld until all the evidence has been examined and all the arguments heard. The judge and jury must be excluded from any partisan role. The partisan role is held by the advocate, whose function is to present the arguments and evidence with a partisan zeal not subject to the restraints of judicial office; his task is not to decide but to persuade.[4]

This excellent description needs to be amplified and emphasized. Under the adversary system, the role of the judge (in the hearing stage) is basically that of supervisor of the proceedings. He ensures that the parties stay within certain boundaries prescribed by law. The prosecution of the case, however, follows the principle of *Parteibetreib* (party prosecution), to use the terminology of German jurisprudence. Party prosecution contrasts with "judicial prosecution," in which the judge does much more than enforce the rules of combat.[5] Under the adversary system it is basically up to the parties, and not the judge, to determine what evidence (or counter-evidence) is presented, what arguments (or counterarguments) are to be made, and how they are going to be presented and made. In general, the court takes no step except on the motion of a party; it is not the business of the judge to see that a party acts in his own interest or makes the most persuasive case he can. In speaking of the parties, however, it should be emphasized that we really mean the parties' representatives, lawyers, professional advocates. The adversary system has been described as an extension of trial by combat, with lawyers playing the role of professional champions. Representation by active partisan professionals and party prosecution are the hallmarks of the adversary system.

What is the justification for the adversary system? Why adopt this method for determining answers to the disputed questions of fact? There appear to be three main justifications offered in its favor, each of which involves a particular outlook on the relationship of the adversary system to justice. For convenience I shall label these respective justifications as the truth-finding theory, the satisfaction theory, and the protection theory.

1. *The truth-finding theory.* This is the traditional position and deserves most of our attention. According to this view, since the decision of the controverted issue depends on answering questions of fact, the trial process should be devoted to truth finding. Jerome Frank cites a modern judge who asserts that "a trial under our procedure is not a game or battle of wits but a painstaking, orderly inquiry for the discovery of truth."[6] And truth, as Lord Eldon wrote in the eighteenth century, is best discovered "by powerful statements on both sides of the question." Another way of stating this position is that an adversarial trial promotes decisions that are well grounded on both the law and the facts because each side will, with partisan zeal, bring to the court's attention all the material favorable to that side, and, therefore, no relevant consideration will escape its notice.

The theory has two components. The first consists of a certain conception of the trial process: it claims that one of the main purposes of a trial is the discovery of truth on the disputed questions of fact. The second component consists of a claim about the adversary system: it states that the adversary system is the best method, or at least a good method, for discovering the truth.

The truth-finding conception of the trial process rests on the connection it perceives between legal justice and truth. It argues that the disposition of a case according to the applicable law of a system presupposes that correct answers are given to the disputed questions of fact. If a case is decided on wrong answers, the case is (legally speaking) wrongly decided, with the result that one of the parties is not given his legal due. A finding of correct answers to the disputed questions of fact is therefore a necessary condition for doing legal justice. A similar connection holds between truth and justice in the moral sense. Thus, if the applicable law in a case is also a just law according to some moral standard, then a decision made on wrong answers to the disputed questions of fact is also morally unjust, and one of the parties is not being given what moral justice requires. (If the applicable law is morally unjust, moral justice will not necessarily be served by discovering the truth on the disputed issues. But it would be odd to conclude that the finding of wrong answers is then an essential purpose of the trial process.)

This argument carries a high degree of persuasiveness. Although it has some problems, it is difficult to see how anyone can entirely reject the view that truth finding is one of the essential purposes of the trial process. In addition, it is hard to see why a society should expend funds to support a system of public courts unless it expects its laws to be enforced. Laws are enforced only when correct answers are given to the questions of fact in a case. Nevertheless, there are doubts that are not easy to put down. It just does not seem plausible to hold that every (and perhaps even any) judicial trial of issues of fact really does succeed in discovering the whole truth, that impeccably correct answers are found on the questions of fact. The doubts that recently have been aired by such distinguished analysts as Judge Marvin Frankel of the U.S. District Court for the Southern District of New York turn on this point.[7]

Let us look at the second component of the truth-finding theory and see if there is some way of quelling these doubts. Is the adversary system a good method for discovering truth on disputed questions of fact? One answer, which may be called the "strong" reply, seems to supply a way of overcoming the problem. It maintains that the adversary system is actually constitutive of truth finding in the trial context. (This seems to be the position advanced some years ago by Stephen Toulmin in his book *The Uses of Argument.)* The argument here is that the law has its own standards or criteria of truth, and its own definition of "truth." The true answer, in law, to a question of fact is by definition that which is decided upon as a consequence of an adversary proceeding—a proceeding in which assertions and counterassertions are subjected to vigorous testing by the parties, each party having a strong stake in the court's rejection of his opponent's assertions. This argument can be strengthened by adopting a Kelsenian theory, which holds that legal norms are hypotheticals: if certain facts exist, then a specific result ought to follow. But the facts in point are, Kelsen holds, always judicial facts, the facts found by the court, and not the so-called true facts in any extralegal sense. What a law says is that if certain facts are judicially found to exist, then a specific result ought to follow. The assignment of rights by a judge is a jural act following upon a finding of the judicial facts.

This seems correct, but the above argument clearly will not suffice, for it proves too much. A similar argument could be constructed for any method of truth finding that might be used in the trial process (such as a nonadversarial method like judicial prosecution or the use of independent investigators). The entire force of the argument, as an argument specifically for the adoption of the adversary system, rests upon the weaker claim that the adversary system is a good method of truth finding, that the critical interrogation of assertions by partisan opponents achieves, or at least approaches, truth in its ordinary meaning.[8] To put the matter in another way, this weaker claim amounts to saying that the adversary system is an efficient method for getting the best answers humanly possible in the trial context, or at least no worse answers than would be gotten through any other method that it would be reasonable to employ in trials. (We should keep in mind that a trial court cannot put off reaching a decision, as the scientific investigator can because all the facts are not in or because unclarities still remain.) The connection perceived as holding between truth and justice would then be reformulated to state that a finding of the best answers to the disputed questions of fact is a necessary condition for doing justice. None of this means that discovery of truth should not be our ideal, for otherwise we might fall into adopting too easy a notion of what is the best we can humanly do. It is vitally important, as Judge Frankel maintains, that truth should not be rated low on the scale of legal values. The acceptance of truth as a basic value may, therefore, dictate modifications in the adversary system where it turns out to be obstructive of truth finding. But this raises problems that we shall have to consider later on.

But is the adversary system a good method? Do adversarial trials of questions of fact promote well-grounded decisions?

In order to see the problem in proper perspective, it is important to recognize that proponents of the adversary system are not unmindful of the difficulties it faces in discovering or approaching truth.[9] Sources of information (witnesses, documents) are not only frequently incomplete but also frequently subjective. Moreover, societal as well as individual assumptions and values introduce both conscious and unconscious distortions in the minds of judges, jurors, and witnesses. To deal with the fallibility of testimony and in part to counter bias, the adversarial trial relies on cross-examination, the "revered rectifier of purposeful fabrication and unwitting error." It is nevertheless clear that the fallibility of testimony and bias are not always remedied by cross-examination.

These admitted difficulties do not appear to devastate the claim that the adversary system is a good method of truth finding or truth approaching, but they do compel the concession that the system is far from foolproof. In their book *The Trial of the Future,* Justice Bernard Botein and Murray Gordon suggest that the adversary system might someday be replaced by laboratory techniques.[10] Drugs that induce recall and disclosure may be more dependable than current testimonial practices and cross-examination. But it is doubtful that such techniques would overcome all the above difficulties. The individual mental set of witnesses and the societal assumptions of judges and jurors could still occasion distortions.

A more far-reaching attack on the adversary system is presented by the late Jerome Frank in his aptly named book *Courts on Trial.* (It is a bit surprising that Frank is so much ignored in current discussions.) Judge Frank is a "fact skeptic." The traditional analysis of judicial decision, says Frank, has focused upon upper (appellate) courts and has concerned itself with uncertainties of the law that arise from difficulties in law finding; it has almost completely overlooked the more radical uncertainties inherent in truth discovery at the trial court level. Here the difficulties in predicting the outcome in a case arise not so much from uncertainty as to which legal rules are applicable but rather as to the facts that will be found. Even if the adversary system were a fairly good method of truth finding, justice would require that it be replaced or modified if some better method were available.

Frank's critique of the present adversary system centers on two points, competence and trial conduct. On the first, Frank plausibly argues that lawyers, judges, and jurors are not especially competent as inquirers into truth or as weighers of evidence. It seems to him totally irrational that they should generally not be required to have a specialist's knowledge on the issues of a case. He therefore proposes that courts be aided in their search for truth by expert, impartial government investigators. This proposal would have two important effects on the trial process: it would to some extent subordinate the judge to the expert, and it would to some extent (and perhaps considerably) restrict the operation of the principle of party prosecution. Still, interestingly enough, Frank does not see his proposal as leading to the complete abolition of the adversary system. A trial should be adversarial as far as possible, for it has some value as a method of truth finding and as a device for protecting the interests of the parties.

It is, however, not easy to discern the shape of the new system that Frank would support. The two essentials of the adversary system, party prosecution and active partisan representation, are in fact quite difficult to disentangle from one another. Control over what facts are to be determined, how evidence is to be collected, and the manner in which evidence is to be presented at the trial (all substantially in the hands of the parties and the advocates) are so interconnected that any alteration at any point in the name of more rational truth finding is bound to have its effects at the other points. The indefiniteness that pervades Judge Frank's apparently "mixed" system of adversariness and nonadversariness seems also to characterize Judge Frankel's present thinking on the matter, though to be perfectly fair, Judge Frankel insists that he is mainly airing doubts about the adversary system, not presenting solutions.

As biting as Frank is on the question of competence, he is even more vigorous in his attack on the way in which the adversarial trial is conducted. He quotes with sarcasm the claim that a trial is "an orderly inquiry for the discovery of truth." On the contrary, says Frank, trial tactics are not geared to the discovery of truth; the lawyer aims at victory, not at aiding the court in discovering the facts. So much is even admitted in the oft-quoted words of Lord Brougham in the trial of Queen Caroline:

> ... An advocate, in this discharge of his duty, knows but one person in all the world, and that person is his client. To save that client by all means and expedients, and at all hazards and costs to other persons, and, amongst them to himself, is his first and only duty; and in performing this duty he must not regard the alarm, the torments, the destruction which he may bring upon others. Separating the duty of a patriot from that of an advocate, he must go on reckless of the consequences, though it should be his unhappy fate to involve his country in confusion.[11]

The adversary system appears to adopt one of the definitions of "justice" Socrates criticized in the first book of the *Republic:* justice is helping your friends and harming your enemies. The "martial spirit," which Frank sees as dominating the trial process, manifests itself in the attempt to secure a favorable jury, in the coaching of witnesses, and in the concealment of evidence that might adversely affect one's case. Cases are decided, says Frank, less on the preponderance of evidence than on the "preponderance of the perjury."[12] Canon Seven of the Code of Professional Responsibility of the American Bar Association prescribes that "a lawyer should represent a client zealously within the bounds of the law." In practice, this zealous representation hardly appears consistent with "an orderly inquiry for the discovery of truth."[13]

Frank's attack seems to have a good deal of validity, but he did not see it as entailing the complete abolition of the adversary system. He pointed out that the system "contains a core of good sense" and has "invaluable qualities with which we cannot afford to dispense."[14] Frank in fact acknowledges that his attack was blunted by the introduction of such reforms in criminal and civil procedure as the public defender and pretrial discovery. To these we may add the pretrial conference. Pretrial discovery and the pretrial conference are designed, in part, to reduce gamesmanship and minimize the use of surprise as a trial tactic and thereby raise the quality of procedural fairness. These reforms are quite understandable if we keep in mind that according to the first component of the truth-finding theory, the discovery of truth—correct or better answers to the disputed questions of fact—is an essential purpose of the trial process. Clearly the purposes of the trial may well dictate modifications in the adversary system. And these modifications may have to be more than structural or formal. I am alluding, of course, to the problem of the ethics of lawyering and ultimately to the ethos of our legal system. (It might be noted that the issues of adversarial ethics that have been discussed by such recent writers as Judge Frankel and Dean Monroe Freedman are not entirely new.[15] Quintilian, for example, was much concerned to rebut ethical critiques of the art of rhetoric. He maintained that in certain cases, it "is not the fault of the art, but of the man."[16] It is debatable, of course, how far this fine distinction holds up.)

2. *The satisfaction theory.* This theory is widely held, yet it is difficult to find any systematic statement of it. It justifies the adversary system in terms of the psychological satisfaction that it gives to the parties in a case, in particular, "the sense of having had a day in court." Martin Mayer quoted the legal researcher Maxine B. Virtue as saying that the litigant's sense of having had a day in court is "close to the heartbeat of justice."[17] Perhaps the most explicit statement of the theory is to be found in the popular *It's Your Law* by the eminent lawyer Charles P. Curtis. In many respects Curtis takes the same position as Monroe Freedman on questions of professional ethics occasioned by the adversary system.

As with the truth-finding theory, the satisfaction theory also has two components: a claim about some essential purpose of trials, a purpose that implicates a view of justice, and a claim that the adversary system promotes that purpose. Curtis tends to discount the connection that the truth-finding theorists have perceived as holding between truth and justice. "Justice," he says, "is something larger and more intimate than truth. Truth is only one of the ingredients of justice. Its whole is the satisfaction of those concerned."[18] The "those concerned" here referred to are not only the parties but also the public (who after all pay for the court system). But, according to Curtis, the public ought to be satisfied if the parties are. As to truth finding, Curtis maintains that the administration of justice is no more designed to elicit truth than science is designed to extract justice from the atom. This point is further buttressed by the consideration that "trial courts are more usually concerned with conflicting characterizations of the facts than with the facts themselves."[19] That is to say, the lawyer's art aims at persuading the court to accept a certain version of what happened; the question of what did happen is usually less in dispute.

Curtis's point about the court's concern with conflicting characterizations of fact is well taken. Questions of negligence, drunkenness, cruelty, provocation, self-defense, and so forth are not straightforward questions of fact. But this hardly constitutes an overwhelming objection to a truth-finding conception of the trial process, for the answers to such questions may very well depend on answers to other questions that are factual in nature. It may well be the case that some of the trial tactics deplored by Judges Frank and Frankel, who are more committed to a truth-finding conception of the purpose of trials, would be allowable in regard to the presentation of argument on how the facts should be characterized. Curtis's position on truth finding is puzzling, in any event. On the one hand he admits that truth is an ingredient of justice, while on the other hand he asserts that the administration of justice is not designed to elicit truth. It is not easy to see on what basis Curtis can explain the reforms of the adversary system that we noted above. It is even more difficult for me to see how a truth-finding conception of the trial process can be so underplayed if the enforcement of laws, and just laws, requires correct or better answers to the disputed questions of fact. Why should the public pay for a system of dispute settling in accordance with rules of law if the rules are not enforced in the process?

But let us pass over these difficulties and turn to the second component of the theory, that the adversary system "gives the algebraic maximum of satisfaction to both parties," as Curtis says, by encouraging them "to fight it out and dissolve their differences in dissension ... combat is one way to justice."[20] From this claim, Curtis derives certain of the features of the adversary system, especially that the advocate must say the best, and only the best, of his own case: and he discusses some of the ethical issues to which this gives rise (for example, whether an attorney may conceal evidence detrimental to his case and whether he ever may be duty-bound to lie for his client). In general Curtis's position is like Dean Freedman's: the lawyer's obligation to his client is greater than his duty to aid the court in the search for truth.

What shall we say of this justification for the adversary system? Are there grounds for believing that the system does promote the "algebraic maximum of satisfaction" for both parties? Does it give the losing party "as much satisfaction as a loser can expect?"[21] Martin Mayer, for one, writes: "Losing litigants after any procedure do not normally feel they have been near the heartbeat of justice; they feel they have been rooked, however elaborate the hearing; if they thought 'justice' called for them to lose, they would have never gone to court in the first place ... too much depends on the skill of the advocates and the luck of the draw."[22] These remarks, if correct, cast considerable doubt on the satisfaction theory: a losing litigant is not likely to feel satisfied.

The issue, however, is more complicated. Through it is true that a losing litigant in an adversarial trial is never very satisfied, the main question is whether he is more satisfied (or less dissatisfied) than he would have been had he lost in a nonadversary adjudicatory proceeding or in some other mode of dispute settlement (including modes in which "losing" means getting less than what one believes one is entitled to). But it is not easy to see how evidence might be garnered on this matter. To be sure, we like to think that an individual feels all the better for having lost in a fair fight, a fair trial, rather than in one that has been rigged to an extent because of some degree of unfairness in the process. But this common belief would be supportive of the satisfaction justification only if it were also the case that the adversary system is a necessary ingredient in a fair trial. I am not certain, however, that this claim is part of Curtis's position, though it might very well be. It would be a curious paradox, at any rate, if the adversary system were a necessary ingredient in a fair trial and, at the same time, the lawyer's obligation to his client permitted ethically questionable conduct.

In any case, whether a loser has the sense of having had "a day in court," and to that extent feels some degree of satisfaction, depends a good deal on whether his lawyer was competent, meaning not competence in truth-discovery methods (as was the case in our discussion of Judge Frank) but rather competence in the law and in courtroom skills. Competence in this latter sense is acknowledged as a serious problem in the United States and Canada. Many jurisdictions are now moving toward required continuing-education courses for lawyers. The Minnesota Supreme Court has recently by order established the first formal program of continuing education for lawyers in the nation (forty-five hours of courses every three years). The question of lawyers' competence at trial work has recently been headlined in the press.[23] An incompetent attorney can rob the client of "a day in court."

The issue of competence is significant not only for the satisfaction theory but also for the other justifications of the adversary system. On any theory of the adversary system the lawyers should be competent in the law and in trial skills. One may be inclined to go even further and say that if a trial is to be fair, the lawyers should be equal in competence, or at least not too disparate in respect to competence. When either of these conditions of competence and rough equality of competence is not met, the judge will be faced with a serious problem regarding procedural justice. A judge should always be neutral, impartial, toward the parties, but a neutral stance will be difficult to maintain if one of the lawyers shows himself to be incompetent or grossly unequal to the other lawyer. In earlier describing the adversary system, I said that it was not the business of the judge to ensure that a party acts in his own interest or makes the most persuasive case he can. But if one of the lawyers is not up to this task, the judge may well have to take a more active role in the proceedings and help the lawyer.[24] Otherwise the client will hardly feel that he has had a day in court and, irrespective of his feelings, the public might not think he has had his day. Should a litigant have to suffer because he had the misfortune (perhaps because he lacked the monetary fortune) to hire an incompetent lawyer or one who is not as good as his opponent's? On the other hand, if the judge takes on a more active role and helps one of the lawyers, the other party is hardly likely to feel that he has had "a day in court." Competence, or rather incompetence, clearly poses a dilemma for a conscientious judge. This problem is not new. The twelfth-century philosopher and jurist Moses Maimonides, writing in the framework of a rather different legal system with a different kind of procedure, makes reference to the problem in his code (*Mishneh Torah,* Book of Judges, XXI, 11).

I am not persuaded that the adversary system gives the losing party "as much satisfaction as a loser can expect," though it may give him all that he is entitled to expect. In any case, the first component of the theory should not be dismissed completely. Curtis may be right in claiming that "justice" has a deeper meaning to which the satisfaction of all those concerned is central. But it is debatable whether this deeper meaning has any relevance to the criminal trial. Curtis's satisfaction theory may have in fact been intended to apply more to the civil trial than to the criminal, but in private disputes it is doubtful that the satisfaction of the parties is best promoted by adjudication (adversarial or otherwise) rather than some other mode of settlement.

3. *The protection theory.* The protection theory may be put in terms of two components. The first maintains that, irrespective of whether a trial aims at truth discovery or something else, justice requires that the parties be given a fair trial of their cause. This means that the rights, especially the procedural rights, of the litigant or defendant should be protected throughout the proceedings. The second component occurs in strong and weak forms. The strong form maintains that the adversary system is a necessary ingredient in a fair trial; a fair trial is an adversarial trial. The weak form maintains that the rights of litigants and defendants are best protected under the adversary system, a system in which each side is represented by a partisan advocate. Professor Lon Fuller, upon whom I earlier drew for my characterization of the adversary system, adds the further point that this system enables us to preserve the integrity of society and its decisions of condemnation, for no one will be condemned as a criminal or civil wrongdoer except through a procedure in which his rights have been protected. The principle that even the guilty have a right to legal representation is actually derived from this consideration, as Fuller argues.

The first component of the protection theory—justice requires a fair trial and protection of procedural rights—is so clear that little needs to be said over and above the mere statement of it. In the United States there has been a shift back toward the adversarial

trial in the juvenile courts because the nonadversarial type of proceeding, which has until recently prevailed, has entailed an invasion
of the rights of the accused (and often of others as well) of the sort
that would not be tolerated in litigation of an adversary type. It is
also clear that if the laboratory techniques to which I earlier referred
should ever be adopted, it might be vital to retain something like the
adversary system, for otherwise there would be grave dangers of
brainwashing and fabrication of evidence.

The strong form of the second component implied that a nonadversarial trial cannot be a fair one. Some writers, and Dean
Freedman seems to be one of them, hold that the U.S. constitutional requirement of due process is satisfied only by the adversary
system, and I do not doubt that this view could be buttressed by an
ample supply of judicial dicta. Fair trial procedure does demand
that no one should be judge in his own cause, that the judge should
have no private interest in the outcome, that the judge should not be
biased, that each party should be given fair notice of the proceedings, that the judge should hear both sides, that a party should not
be heard in private, that each party should have the opportunity to
respond to the arguments and evidence of the other party, that the
decision should be supportable by reasons, and that the reasons
should take into account the argument and evidence presented.[25] I
am inclined to believe that some degree of adversariness is a necessary element in a fair trial, but how large a degree is a very difficult
question. I do not know enough about the continental nonadversary
systems to be in a position to say that they entirely exclude adversariness. I am also inclined to think that party prosecution could be
considerably diminished without compromising fairness.

If this is the case, the protection theory turns on the second version of the second component: the adversary system is still the
best way of protecting a defendant's procedural rights, or (even
more weakly) at least a good way of protecting these rights. I suppose it must be conceded that it does a good job of this, because the
complaint against the adversary system by Judges Frank and
Frankel is that it does too good a job, so that the search for truth
suffers in the process. This result is to some extent inevitable,
given rules of procedure based on the social decision that it is better
that a guilty person should be exonerated than an innocent man be

convicted. But to what lengths may an advocate go in protecting his client? This question brings up all the issues of professional ethics. Certainly the prosecutor has no excuse to avoid a duty (moral and legal) to aid the court in its search for the truth. Certainly the adversarial ethos of the lawyer encourages, if it does not exactly license, ethically questionable conduct to the point, for example, of subtly coaching the accused and the witnesses in the art of perjury. But it is not easy to see how a defense attorney's role could be made into a more collaborative truth-seeking role without raising doubts in the client's mind as to where his lawyer's loyalties lie. One recoils at the view expressed by law professors at the University of Havana that "the first job of a revolutionary lawyer is not to argue that his client is innocent, but rather to determine if his client is guilty and, if so, to seek the sanction which will best rehabilitate him."[26] This is a burlesque of the truth-finding conception of the purpose of trials, of course, but to what extremes of adversarial process need we go in order to avoid this burlesque?

If we are to preserve a commitment to truth finding and to protecting rights, since both are requirements of justice, it would seem that some modification of the adversary system is called for. The modification of the commitment to discover the truth has already been made to a degree, for example, in the adoption of the exclusionary rules. Judge John Sirica to the contrary not withstanding, it is not correct to say that a trial aims solely at the t-r-u-t-h. If truth were the only aim, we might be justified in using torture. The fact is that there are truth-concealing rules, such as the privilege against self-incrimination, as well as truth-discovery rules. But any modification of party prosecution and partisan representation would seem to have ripple effects all down the line. Perhaps we must abide the unhappy conclusion that there are two irreconcilable conceptions of courthouse justice: the trial judge's, which sees it as truth finding, and the trial (defense) lawyer's, which sees it as protecting rights. This is not so much corruption in the palace of justice as it is paradox.

The protection theory has its practical difficulties. One assumes that the advocate is going to do his best for his client. But is this necessarily the case? Does the lawyer always aim at victory? Abraham Blumberg has argued that when a criminal defendant is poor and also very likely guilty, his lawyer's aim is not so much to win the case as to make sure he collects his fee. The courts and the criminal bar, says Blumberg, are actually engaged in a big "confidence game."[27] This may be an extreme accusation, but if there is any truth to it, it surely constitutes a difficulty in practice to the protection theory.

There are difficulties in principle, too, if we think of the protection theory as primarily a supplement to the other justifications of the adversary system. It is not easy to see how we can design a dispute-settling process that enforces the law, preserves the integrity of society, protects the rights of litigants and defendants, gives one a sense of having had a day in court, and protects the interests of all others who may be involved in the process (such as witnesses), as speedily and as cheaply as possible![28]

## Notes

1. The answer presented here is an idealized account that enables treatment of the essentials of the problem of the justification of the adversary system in this space. Numerous fine points and qualifications are therefore elided. To some extent my opening sentence is itself an oversimplification, for in some proceedings certain facts are stipulated and the remaining disputed issue, for instance, concerns the characterization of the facts (for example, whether the conduct in question was reasonable). The traditional view, at any rate, covers the run-of-the-mill adversarial trial.
2. Karl N. Llewellyn, *The Bramble Bush* (New York: Oceana Publications, 1951), p. 43.
3. For a treatment see my *Philosophy of Law* (Englewood Cliffs, N.J.: Prentice-Hall, 1975), chap. 6.
4. "The Adversary System," in *Talks on American Law*, ed. H. J. Berman (New York: Vintage Books, 1961), pp. 30ff.
5. For a suggestive comparison of adversary and nonadversary procedure, see Mirjan Damaška, "Presentation of Evidence and Factfinding Precision," *University of Pennsylvania Law Review* 123 (1975): 1083-1106.
6. Jerome Frank, *Courts on Trial* (New York: Antheneum, 1963), p. 89 (originally published in 1949).

7. Marvin Frankel, "The Search for Truth: An Umpireal View," *University of Pennsylvania Law Review* 123 (1975): 1031-1059. For a critique, see the article in same issue by Monroe Freedman, "Judge Frankel's Search for Truth," pp. 1060-1066.

8. I grant that truth in its ordinary meaning is not at issue in every trial. The parties' dispute may concern only the question of what the law is, in which event a somewhat modified treatment of the justification of the adversary system would be required. Still, the question of what is the law may in part turn on disputed factual questions or interpretations of facts. See note 1, above.

9. See Jack B. Weinstein, "Some Difficulties in Devising Rules for Determining Truth in Judicial Trials," *Columbia Law Review* 66 (1966): 223-246.

10. Bernard Botein and Murray Gordon, *The Trial of the Future* (New York: Simon and Schuster, 1963), chap. 2.

11. *Trial of Queen Caroline* 8 (1821).

12. Frank, *Courts on Trial,* p. 85.

13. Evidently the topic has a hoary history. Aulus Gellius, *Attic Nights* (I, 6, 4), quotes Titus Castricius: "It is the rhetor's [the trial lawyer's] privilege to make statements that are untrue, daring, crafty, deceptive and sophistical, provided they have some semblance of truth and can by any artifice be made to insinuate themselves into the minds of the persons who are to be influenced."

14. Frank, *Courts on Trial,* pp. 80, 81.

15. See Frankel, "Search for Truth," and Dean Monroe Freedman, *Lawyers' Ethics in an Adversary System* (New York: Oceana Publications, 1975).

16. *Institutes* II, xvii, 40.

17. Martin Mayer, *The Lawyers* (New York: Dell Publ. Co., 1968), p. 457.

18. Charles P. Curtis, *It's Your Law* (Cambridge, Mass.: Harvard University Press, 1954), p. 21.

19. Ibid., p. 85.

20. Ibid., pp. 3, 4.

21. Ibid., p. 21.

22. Mayer, *The Lawyers,* p. 457.

23. See, for example, *Wall Street Journal,* February 24, 1975, p. 1.
24. See Charles D. Breitel, "Ethical Problems in the Performance of the Judicial Function," in *Conference on Judicial Ethics,* University of Chicago Law School Conference Series, no. 19 (1965), pp. 64-81.
25. See Golding, *Philosophy of Law,* chap. 6.
26. Cited in Freedman, *Search for Truth,* p. 1063.
27. Abraham Blumberg, *Criminal Justice* (New York: Law Viewpoints, 1974), pp. 110-115.
28. In addition to the works cited, the following were of special help in preparing this paper: R. W. Millar, "The Formative Principles of Civil Procedure," in A. Engelmann et al., *A History of Continental Civil Procedure* (Boston: Little Brown, 1927), pp. 3-81; Jerome Michael, "The Basic Rules of Pleading," *The Record of the Bar of the City of New York* (1950), pp. 175-201; Jerome Michael and Mortimer Adler, "The Trial of an Issue of Fact," *Columbia Law Review* 34 (1934): 1224-1306, 1462-1493. Unfortunately a suggestive article by Professor Robert S. Summers came into my hands too late to take into account: "Evaluating and Improving Legal Processes—A Plea for 'Process Values,'" *Cornell Law Review* 60 (1974): 1-52.

# 10

# Comment: "On the adversary system and justice"

## ROBERT S. SUMMERS

Professor Golding gives an account of adversarial trial and briefly identifies possible nonadversarial alternatives. He does not systematically consider in what ways the adversarial might be preferred but explores three possible justifications for adversarial trial (mostly without regard to alternatives).

The first justification is what Golding calls the "truth-finding" theory, and I will concentrate on it, as applied to civil cases. Golding does not contend that adversarial trial might be justified as a superior means of ascertaining the truth, merely for the sake of ascertaining the truth. He stresses that the truth must be found if justice is to be done between the parties to a dispute. In general Golding is right. At least if we assume that the rule governing the dispute is itself a just rule—one that yields the just result if applied to the true facts—then the true facts of the dispute must be found if the rule is to yield the just result. If the true facts are not found and the rule is instead applied to false "facts," the result will not be just (except perhaps by occasional happenstance).

Certainly truth is important and in ways and for reasons Golding does not consider (though would likely agree to). He focuses on truth as an avenue to justice (assuming just governing rules). But many legal rules are not concerned with justice. Rather, they are designed to serve public policy goals, such as reduction of pollution, enhancement of highway safety, and child welfare. Assuming these rules are aptly designed (that is, embody appropriate means-goal hypotheses), then the truth must generally be found, too, if such rules are to be applied to serve their goals as contemplated. Many trials are concerned with applying just such rules. Thus, contrary to what Golding intimates, the so-called truth-finding justification for the adversarial system does not exclusively "rely on a particular conception of justice or, more accurately, some facet of the concept of justice." Laws are means to many ends besides justice, and to serve these we must, as Golding puts it, seek "correct answers . . . to the questions of fact in a case." Thus, the adversarial system is a means of ascertaining truth not only for purposes of doing justice, but also for purposes of serving goals of public policy.

Indeed, the rule of law itself is not possible without rule over fact. Disputes over facts relevant to the application of law are inevitable in a legal order. A system that failed to provide some means of authoritatively resolving such disputes more or less faithfully to the truth (in at least a significant proportion of cases) could not even be a legal order. The world of law and the world of fact are not separate worlds. Every rule of law contemplates a state of fact. Law exists to be applied to fact. A law cannot be applied except to an actual or assumed state of fact. And only if the state of fact comports with truth is the law faithfully applied—applied according to the factual requirements of the rules.

If courts did not seek the truth (as called for by the relevant rules), social goal subservience through law would falter badly outside of court too, and thus badly overall. Courts see only a tiny proportion of disputes, as Golding notes. Most social goal subservience necessarily occurs through extra-judicial efforts at self-application of law by private and official addressees. Yet the addressees will be influenced in these out-of-court efforts by how they think relevant issues of fact would likely be resolved if formally tried in court. Thus, it is almost certain that far fewer goals of law would be served through extra-judicial means in a system in which trials were not primarily truth oriented than in one in which they were. In such a system, disputants over issues of fact would have no incentive (or much less incentive) to try to resolve factual issues in accordance with the actual facts (relevant by the terms of the law) and to apply the law accordingly, for the disputing party upholding the version of the facts closest to the truth would rarely be in a position to say to the other that they would then have to go to court so the disputing party could prove he was right about the relevant facts.

Truth is important for another reason. When law is authoritatively applied to an authoritatively determined state of fact (relevant under the law), general propositions supposedly come into contact with concrete reality. If that reality is true reality, the judge (or judges) can test the soundness of the generality against the concrete facts, and, if the generality is found wanting, the judge (or judges) will, at least in common law fields, have power to abandon the generality or to modify it in some way, not only in the case at hand but for the future. Judges in our system are not mere law appliers, they are law creators. If they are to discharge their creative tasks properly, they must formulate law in light of the true facts. If the reality before them is untrue, then their formulations will rest on false factual premises.

If truth (in light of relevant rules) were not the primary object of the trial, the public would probably lose confidence in the process. If the objective of seeking the truth turned out to be pretense, or to be quite secondary, the public would discover this and would almost certainly want to devise trials that were primarily truth oriented, for the public would readily see that there cannot be a rule of law without relevant rule over fact. Yet what would these new trials look like? How could they differ from the present system? Our trials and the rules that constitute and govern them already have truth finding as their primary object. I do not see how new rules could differ, in basic character. (This is not to say existing trials may not be improved.)

If truth is important, how does the adversarial trial fare as a means to the truth? Here, much depends on what Golding means by adversarial trial. Certainly some forms of it are far less truth oriented than others. For example, even with the improvements of the standard civil adversarial trial that Golding mentions, one can still imagine important further improvements that would make our system more truth productive. For example, opposing lawyers might be better matched. And resources for pretrial factual investigation and other forms of investigation might be equalized (at appropriate levels). Rules might be devised to proscribe coaching of witnesses and to downplay gamesmanship, trial tricks, and histrionic theatrics of the lawyers. Provision might be made for trials to be held immediately after events while memories are fresh. With these and still other changes, most of us would be likely to say that the adversarial method at least promises to be a reasonably good method of arriving at truth. It would provide for the careful delineation of the relevant factual issues, in advance. It would afford opposing parties strong incentives to prepare and present the best evidence to support their positions—certainly a stronger incentive than an inquisitional judge acting on his own (or through civil servant investigators) would be likely to have. It would afford fuller opportunity for the presentation and challenge (through cross-examination and other means) of all such evidence than a straight inquisitorial method in which the roles of the opposing parties are vastly diminished. It would institutionalize suspension of judgment on the part of the decision maker until both sides had presented their cases and their respective challenges and rebuttals, and would thus diminish the risk of prejudgment so inherent in more inquisitorial methods. The foregoing constitute strong reasons to suppose that a well-devised adversarial trial would not be merely highly truth oriented but more so than inquisitorial methods. That we do not yet have such a system in itself proves nothing except perhaps that we are not as reform minded as we should be.

No mode of trial—adversarial, inquisitorial, or other—that is exclusively truth oriented should be devised. The rules must make room for other social goals, too, and these will sometimes foreclose inquiry that would lead to discovery of the truth. Our own adversarial system is just such a multipurpose system. (The literature of jurisprudence awaits a systematic account of this central feature of the trial process). Moreover, even if an adversarial setup could be devised that was exclusively truth oriented, it would certainly fail to uncover the truth in a not insignificant proportion of cases. There are uneliminable limits to the efficacy of legal forms (another little understood subject, as yet).

But it does not follow from the multipurpose character of trials or from the inherently limited efficacy of law and legal processes that truth finding either is not or ought not to be the main objective of trials of issues of fact. Simply because the pursuit of truth conflicts with other goals of the process that sometimes take priority, it does not follow that truth is secondary. And simply because we cannot always find the truth, it hardly follows that we ought not to try. Moreover, while our society may actually have devised a mode of trial that fails to yield the truth as often as feasible, this hardly demonstrates that truth is not primary. If truth were not primary, then how else could we understand our trial process and most of the rules defining and governing trials? I submit that the rules can only be intelligibly understood as primarily concerned with the ascertainment of truth. No other single goal similarly runs through them, lends them coherence, and ties them together. Professor Golding would probably agree.

A further possible justification for adversarial trial that Golding does not treat separately but that is cognate to truth finding is what might be called "accuracy of law application." It is, of course, not enough for the trial merely to uncover the true facts. The law must be applied to the facts, too, if the rule of law and relevant particular goals are to be served. And the application of law to fact is itself often the subject of complex disputes. (I do not claim that the two processes of fact finding and law application are wholly separable.)

It is better that a judge hear vigorous opposing legal arguments as to applicable law (in cases of dispute over law at trial) than that the judge rely mainly on his own assumed ability to formulate and carry on vigorous contrapuntal dialogue with himself. Among other things, the adversarial method again relevantly institutionalizes suspension of judgment until all the legal arguments are heard. And it must not be thought that issues as to applicable law are rare in the course of trials. On the contrary, they are common; judges have many occasions to err in determining applicable law. A method, adversarial or other, that minimizes applicational error would therefore be genuinely prizeworthy on this ground.

Golding discusses two further possible justifications for adversarial adjudication: the satisfaction theory and the protection theory. Since most of what I would suggest by way of addition to or possible emendation of these theories is already set forth in my article, "Process Values,"* I say no more.

*Robert S. Summers, "Evaluating and Improving Legal Processes—A Plea for 'Process Values'," *Cornell Law Review* 60 (1974): 1-52.

# 11

# The adversary system

**MORLEY R. GORSKY**

In his introduction to *The Philosophy of Law*, R. M. Dworkin refers to "the familiar assumption that the philosophy of law is a discipline separate from the practice of law."[1] By his choice of essays Dworkin endeavors to cast doubt on this assumption, which is consistent with his view that "the philosophy of law studies philosophical problems raised by the existence and *practice of law*."[2] Practicing lawyers do not doubt that they have something important to contribute when an examination is made of the practice of law. This sentiment would apply to examinations made by philosophers and legal academics with an interest in the philosophy of law. Unfortunately, for the latter two groups, they rarely draw upon the practicing lawyer's experience with the subject of their examination. As a result of my twenty-four years' experience as a lawyer as both a practitioner and then as a full-time academic, this situation is a source of great disappointment.

When I attempt to relate my experience as an advocate before the courts and its effect on my understanding of the adversary system, particularly to philosophers of law, I have often found that we fail to communicate. If Dworkin is correct, who is the philosopher to consult about the practice of law for his insights into that area of his concern? Among the other available sources (the parties to litigation, judges, legal literature) I would hope that the practicing lawyer's perspective will not be ignored.

As a discipline exercise I have no fundamental quarrel with Dr. Golding's article. He acknowledges the difficulties in the protection theory, which are a result of the inability to secure evidence, but he does not enlarge his observations to include the effect of this deficiency on both the satisfaction theory and the truth-finding theory. I recognize that there is ample precedent for largely ignoring the law, when examining a problem related to the philosophy of law, and Golding has demonstrated how this can be done with a good result—as has Professor Summers in his commentary. I suggest that there is also room for an examination of the philosophical problems raised by the adversarial system that treats the practitioner's experience as having great significance.

The major difficulty in bringing lawyers and philosophers of law together in discourse is in the nature of the two disciplines. Because the study of the philosophy of law is necessarily devoted to various methods of philosophy and only to a lesser extent with law in its traditional setting, certain limitations in the ability to communicate must develop.

It is now much more the case than it was even twenty years ago for lawyers, both academic and practicing ones, to restrict themselves to a specialty. With the proliferation of new developments in law, it has become increasingly difficult for lawyers to communicate with each other when they cross lines of specialization. Such being the case, how are lawyers and philosophers of law to communicate with each other where a specialist's knowledge of law or philosophy is required to enable free communication?

Needless to say, I fall into the category of lawyer absent formal credentials in philosophy; however, I hope my comments will not be treated as a nonphilosopher's blanket criticism of the approach to law that philosophers of law take. Quite apart from the difficulty of attaining a lawyer's specialized understanding of the functioning of a legal system and at the same time maintaining standing as a philosopher, such heroic endeavors seem unnecessary. In assuming the philosopher's role, it is apparently usual to make certain assumptions concerning the concepts of law and justice and the nature of the society being considered which reduce one's reliance on "facts" and "propositions," as the lawyer more usually understands them. An example is John Rawls's *A Theory of Justice*, where the subject of the principles of justice is discussed, after restricting the scope of inquiry so that it is unnecessary to consider law as the lawyer or client functioning in the world of practice experiences it.[3] In fact, I cannot recall any reference to legal theory in a conventional setting as it might affect Rawls's theories.

Similarly, Joseph Raz has observed that a consideration of the

laws of a particular society has "not figured greatly in jurispru-
dential discussions."[4] But where such laws become relevant, as in
the process of answering the preliminary question, Does a legal
system exist in a certain society? a knowledge of that law and its
functioning becomes imperative.

This need is to be contrasted with the position Raz took in his
book's introduction that the theory of a legal system ought to proceed in the absence of much attention to problems of content. He
chose to develop his systematic conclusions "largely through the
critical examination of previous theories," and accordingly found it
convenient "to disregard [content] almost exclusively."[5]

I therefore suggest that where the philosopher of law bases his
theories and conclusions upon a universe that is not constructed
merely to serve as a model for the philosopher's theory of justice,
then there is a real danger that the work will suffer from such errors
as are exposed. When a theory of justice is based upon empirical
evidence, and it turns out that the observations relied upon suffer
from inaccuracy, lawyers (probably most of them) and perhaps
many philosophers would experience some unease in accepting the
conclusions drawn from the evidence mustered. This is more likely
to be the case where the references to the law are intended to be
accurate and are made an essential part of the theory being the subject of exposition. Where a philosopher engages in philosophical
anthropology and where an assessment of a system will be based
on observations and identification of the mechanisms which exist
within that system, then any theory developed will, as F. C. S.
Northrop stated in *Philosophical Anthropology and Practical Politics,* be as good as the method employed.[6] Part of such method will
depend upon an accurate understanding of that system.

I believe that the lawyer, who has an interest in and some appre-
ciation of philosophy, can assist the philosopher of law, whose
approach requires a more reliable knowledge of certain legal facts
and propositions than a philosopher, even if legally trained, can
usually hope to possess. I also hope that the work of lawyers (for
some time such lawyers are likely to be academics) will be able to
benefit from the assistance of philosophers. One need not look far
for areas where lawyers could benefit from such an association. So
much of a lawyer's time is spent in framing and interpreting lan-

guage and so little has been done to acquaint lawyers with the work being done in this area in philosophy that a clear basis for cooperation exists.

And now to the business at hand, the adversary system. My experience in this area is as a practitioner and teacher of the law of procedure and practice in the courts, where the adversary system tends to be accepted without much question. Any attempt to analyze the concept of a trial and to suggest a justification of the adversary system would benefit greatly from an understanding of the process, not only as it is usually represented but as it actually takes place. There is a difference between the image of a trial drawn from descriptions (which can be obtained from the rules of practice and evidence and a reading of the legal literature, including case reports) and the process as it is usually experienced by those involved. To a considerable extent the written material presumes the existence of conventions, much as Rawls makes assumptions that provide a framework for his theory. While it may be acceptable in formulating a theory to say, "If my grandmother had wheels she would be a streetcar," it certainly would not be so where a reliance is placed on empirical data. In the case of the adversary system, the literature—especially reports of decided cases and the rules of practice and works on the law of evidence, which have major roles in shaping the system—obscures the existence of elements that affect the functioning of the system. This seems to me to be fundamental to a philosophical study of the adversary system, which is related to the practice of law and not only to the existence of law.

The reality of the trial is that, especially in cases decided by a judge alone (which is the usual Anglo-Canadian experience), the outcome of a case is dependent on the parties' ability to bring out facts which will require a determination that supports their position. Without wishing to reduce in importance the subject of the substantive law, it is difficult to refute Jerome Frank's conclusion that the substantive law causes considerably less difficulty in the litigation process than does the subject matter of the trial upon which the questions of law will be decided.[7]

Problems of proof of the facts that comprise the essential elements without which the desired conclusion of law cannot be reached comprise the most important factor in making the adversary system acceptable to those who regard relative equality as necessary for the effective functioning of a system of adjudication. Unlike Frank, I am not immediately concerned with the role that the lawyers for the adversaries may play in subverting those tendencies within the adversary system for bringing forth an accurate reproduction of the facts. By the term "accurate reproduction of the facts" I do not necessarily mean the true facts, which Charles Curtis would treat as unessential,[8] but what the parties honestly believe to represent the true facts. If certain facts exist and a party to the litigation concludes that they form part of Frank's formula (Fact + Law = the Decision), that would be appropriate in his case; to the extent that the adversary system interferes with his adducing such facts in evidence, the system falls short of realizing its potential as an engine for justice.

To the extent that the system deprives a litigant of a reasonable possibility of obtaining and adducing relevant evidence it must be held deficient. Because the literature, which records the result of litigation and the reasons for the decision (the reports), and the rules, which govern the conduct of litigation (rules of procedure and evidence), do not usually reflect this problem, it is often overlooked. Certainly those who, like Frank, consider this factor vital have not been very successful in provoking further jurisprudentially oriented studies of the role of procedure in the process of fact determination in adversarial litigation. I may be beating a dead horse but this is the essence of my experience. If my perceptions thus far are correct they may be considered as being too elementary to be of any value to the philosopher.

Such exposure as the general public has to the process of litigation (usually as observers) may not disclose the difficulties imposed by the system on the production of relevant evidence. All that the lay observer usually sees is the end product of litigation—the trial. There is an assumption that the parties adduce the evidence that they have chosen to adduce and in the manner (subject to objection) that suits them. The reality is very often quite different. Problems of obtaining and adducing evidence pose difficulties of varying degree. Nevertheless, there are a number of problems that can serve as examples.

1. When an essential witness is reluctant to testify (and assum-

ing that the evidence to be given will be based upon honest recollection), it is not possible to compel the witness to speak to the lawyer for the party intending to call him, although it is possible, in most jurisdictions, to subpoena the witness to appear at trial and testify on the behalf of the party who has obtained the subpoena. In some jurisdictions it is possible to compel the attendance of the witness and to obtain a sworn statement. This procedure has the appearance of fairness, but it overlooks the fact that such a witness is often unreliable. To compel a litigant to undertake the risk of calling such a witness, without some safeguards, can result in considerable unfairness. Given the almost universal restraints imposed upon impeaching one's own witness, the possibility of having the recalcitrant witness decide to testify in accordance with what he has previously stated is a remote one.

There is a not infrequent disinclination for a person to become involved as a witness in the court proceedings even where the only request is that the witness recount the facts as he recalls them. Reasons for such reluctance could include concern about whether one's recollections may be shown to be false on cross-examination, a desire not to lose time from work and consequent loss of wages, fear of retribution, fear of a strange environment, or fear of lawyers.

To some it might appear that this problem could be overcome, or at least lessened, if the witness could be examined by a court-appointed functionary. Counsel for the parties could be given the opportunity to question the witness, and the usual rules concerning impeachment of one's own witness would not apply. The witness would not feel dragged by one of the antagonists into a controversy not of his making, as he would be a witness for neither of the parties. Apart from inconvenience, the witness would not lose any wages if his testimony was taken after working hours.

To the extent that such a means was made available for examining an otherwise reluctant and perhaps hostile witness (not necessarily in the legal sense) and thereby overcome a possible loss of necessary evidence, the adversary system would have been made to conform more closely with the inquisitorial system associated with civil law jurisdictions. At the same time certain elements of the adversarial system would be preserved if counsel for the parties were permitted to cross-examine the witness. Such a right is curtailed under the civil law system, and support for this is subject to certain reservations.

Sometimes this type of witness can be induced to give evidence voluntarily but only when his initial fears have been assuaged, often after a considerable expenditure of time on the part of counsel. It is a maxim among lawyers that a lawyer has nothing to sell but his time. Consequently the litigant of modest means may not be able to secure a reluctant witness, while the affluent litigant will have an advantage. Similarly demands for prospective costs of the witness attending, beyond normal mileage and witness fees, can more easily be borne by the affluent litigant. Unless the state is prepared to bear the cost of removing this problem, not only may justice often not be done, it certainly will not appear to be done.

2. A party may be unaware of the existence of potential witnesses. Who saw the accident? When did a particular event occur? Was anyone present? Are relevant documents in existence? Competent investigation is expensive. Who can bear the cost? More likely it will not be the litigant of modest means.

3. Who will secure the services of necessary expert witnesses? Whenever technical, scientific, or trade evidence is called for, the party who fails to tender evidence of this kind reduces his likelihood of success. Many corporate litigants have both the financial resources and a body of available experts who willingly appear as witnesses. A reluctant expert witness is a danger equal to the reluctant nonexpert witness. Furthermore, an expert witness usually expects to be paid more for his time, which will include all time spent related to the case, not just that spent on the witness stand.

Experts furnished and paid for by the state would create a greater sense of equality between the parties. Many jurisdictions permit a judge to call such a person to act as an adviser to the court on technical matters, although some appeal courts have recently criticized the practice as being one that tends to cause the judge to abdicate his role.

4. In most jurisdictions it is considered proper for a lawyer not only to interview a prospective witness but also to review with him the evidence that the witness intends to give at the trial. In addition, the witness will be acquainted with the kinds of question he can expect to be asked in examination-in-chief and in cross-examination.

When such a practice is omitted or too little time is devoted to it, usually because it is most time-consuming and therefore constitutes a contributing factor to the high cost of litigation, the witness's evidence given in court often fails to convey the version of the facts the party calling such witness had reason to anticipate would be forthcoming. To many laymen this would merely represent an example of the lay maxim, "you gambled and lost," while often the difference between the evidence given in court and the statement previously given to counsel can be attributed to the anxiety provoked by the witness's being introduced into a strange and (to the witness) menacing environment and being compelled (without previous assistance) to testify to matters that happened some time ago. Too often the public views the activities of counsel, in his relations with witnesses, as an exercise in bending testimony to serve a partisan purpose. If this really was the case, except in a minority of situations, this exercise might now be terminated and Shakespeare's admonition followed.

To abolish counsel's right to prepare a witness adequately for trial and to justify such abolition as representing a means of promoting equality would do nothing to advance the cause of bringing either the true facts or the parties' honestly held version of the facts before the court. It would only create a sham equality. Nor does the suggested introduction of a state-appointed investigator, who is responsible for examining witnesses, with the parties' counsel being reduced to a secondary role, solve the problem; it only moves it into another arena.

5. There are inept counsel. Very often, however, the ill-prepared counsel, who appears to be inept, is a victim of a system that makes it virtually impossible to prepare his case adequately within existing financial strictures.

The layman will often respond that this problem could be easily overcome by compelling lawyers to prepare a case adequately or else be penalized. This suggestion overlooks the real cost factor involved in properly preparing a case and all of the elements that are included in the preparation. Before the parties appear in court, in a civil case, the lawyer must interview his client to obtain information concerning the matter at hand. Except in the simplest case the interview may take several hours. The facts obtained in the interview ought to be set out in a memorandum, which must then be considered with a view to obtaining further information from the client and setting the stage for an assessment of the client's legal position. Persons who may have information relevant to the matter must be communicated with and arrangements made to interview them and obtain their statements. Documents, and possibly relevant real evidence, that surface during the process of interviewing the client and other persons must be obtained and considered. Where technical matters arise, experts are retained, who must be interviewed and instructed. Reports of experts must be obtained, discussed, and assessed.

Throughout this process additional meetings will often become necessary in order to obtain further advice and instructions. It is only after the clearest statement of facts has thus been obtained that the lawyer can examine these facts in the light of relevant legal authority in order to evaluate the legal position of the client and the available courses of action. When the lawyer has done this, he will again communicate with the client and will advise the client accordingly and request further instructions.

All of the above groundwork will take place before some action in a matter can be properly begun. The time involved in the process will be considerable. Thirty hours is not unusual. How many clients can afford or are willing to undertake the expense of such services for advice alone? But anything less often leads to the giving of inadequate advice. (I emphasize that in outlining the practice to be followed, I am not preaching a practice of perfection.)

If the client gives instructions to commence action and preliminary attempts to obtain redress, short of action, fail, the lawyer must consider the best way to frame the action. Legal work performed hastily, because of financial constraints, can often lead to inadequately drawn pleadings that can seriously affect the client's chance of success.

Pretrial discovery devices serve a useful function in that they permit the obtaining of much information, which might otherwise result in surprise at trial. The client is often involved in these proceedings, and proper preparation necessitates attendances to prepare for questions that might be put to the client. The careful lawyer must consider the questions he intends to ask and their purpose, as well as the questions that may be put by opposing counsel. Transcripts of such pretrial discovery devices are invaluable aids at trial but only if properly indexed and cross-indexed for easy reference. All of this work takes time and adds to the expense of litigation. Documents produced by the opposite party must be obtained, copied, and examined. This important discovery device is often approached in a perfunctory manner because it, too, is time-consuming.

Preparation for trial requires the development of lines of questioning to be employed during examination-in-chief and cross-examination. Alternative questions must be devised, problems of evidence and substantive law anticipated, and solutions to anticipated difficulties drafted. Witnesses must be seen before trial.

All the material to be used at trial must be set out in such a way as to permit an orderly, coherent presentation of the case. Legal argument must be prepared based on as many possible issues as can reasonably be anticipated. Law is much concerned with possibilities. The astute lawyer must be prepared to cope with the possibilities, but his attention to possibilities is similarly time-consuming and therefore expensive. Contrary to current mythology the trial is not such a spontaneous proceeding as pictured in television drama; its course and content are largely based on lengthy and difficult pretrial preparation.

This most attenuated description ought to be sufficient to demonstrate the hazards of skimping on preparation. It also indicates why good preparation is so expensive. Attribution of a number of qualities to the adversary system as a preliminary to development of a philosophical theory concerning the process, without sufficient consideration of the features which I have outlined, can result in flawed conclusions.

I have not attempted to compare the adversary system with its alternatives but have restricted my observations to the limitations of any examination of the adversary system (in the higher civil courts) that fails to reflect the extent to which it adds to inequality, when the system leaves to the parties the responsibility of adducing evidence.

A relatively new factor has been introduced into some jurisdictions by the creation of various state-supported legal aid plans. Because such plans most often provide assistance in criminal litigation and generally benefit the poor, even where ostensibly of universal application (that is, based on the anticipated financial burden and not merely on financial status), the way in which such innovations will affect the ability to seek and produce evidence in civil cases is not yet known. Because of the limits placed on fees paid in cases where the use of private practitioners is permitted, under a legal aid plan, the ability to overcome previous cost limitations may not be very much changed. Where public lawyers serve as legal aid lawyers, they often suffer from an inability to surmount the burden of large case loads and limited funds.

I would also note that any examination of the adversary system of dispute settlement must consider the different ways in which the system exists in and affects the process when different amounts of money are involved; different issues are involved; either civil or criminal litigation is the subject of enquiry; different tribunals are being considered, that is, courts, quasi-judicial boards, administrative boards, and boards of arbitration (my focus has been broadly directed at civil litigation without any real differentiation); it operates in juvenile courts; it operates in family courts.

My comments may appear to have been too much related to the practice of law and too far removed from matters that concern philosophers of law. I trust that my opening statement has provided a satisfactory explanation for my approach. In maintaining this approach I have been influenced by Carl Joachim Friedrich, who observes that philosophers tend to emphasize reliance upon an existing philosophical position while lawyers and jurists incline to an examination which leads to a position. As Friedrich observes, these approaches tend to overlook a view of law and justice, based upon the intimate relationship, in all human experience, of fact and value.[9] This is the position that I have endeavored to support in my commentary.

138    Adjudication

## Notes

1. R. M. Dworkin, ed., *The Philosophy of Law* (London: Oxford University Press, 1977), p. 1.
2. Ibid. (Emphasis added.)
3. See John Rawls, *A Theory of Justice* (Cambridge, Mass.: Harvard University Press, 1972), pp. 7-11.
4. Joseph Raz, *The Concept of a Legal System* (Oxford: Clarendon Press, 1970), pp. 206-207.
5. Ibid., p. 2.
6. See F. C. S. Northrop, *Philosophical Anthropology and Practical Politics* (Portland, Ore.: Old Oregon, 1960).
7. See Jerome Frank, *Courts on Trial* (New York: Atheneum, 1963).
8. See Charles P. Curtis, *It's Your Law* (Cambridge, Mass.: Harvard University Press, 1954).
9. See Carl Joachim Friedrich, *The Philosophy of Law in Historical Perspective,* rev. ed. (Chicago: University of Chicago Press, 1963).

# Part IV.                    PRIVACY

# 12

# Introduction

**DAVID FLAHERTY**

Privacy sells newspapers and builds careers. Data protection spawns new companies and publications. A new field of civil litigation is growing rapidly. Academics and politicians spur on their careers by worrying about the meaning of personal privacy. But even such serious thinkers on the subject are reluctant to tarry long over definitions. It is not simple to describe what privacy means to particular persons living in a specific national culture in the years leading up to 1984. One turns to the following papers by philosophers of law with particular hopes of wringing from them a more tangible sense of the meaning and value of privacy.

One of the best things about Professor Wasserstrom's essay is that it is not about the law, or especially about the law of privacy. It is a discussion of privacy as a human and personal value and of its importance in everyday life. Courts in Western societies too rarely confront the essential meaning of privacy in Wasserstrom's human terms. In the first half of his essay he is concerned about a relatively primitive form of invasion of privacy by means of the interception of conversations. Western law has intervened to impose controls here, especially regarding wiretaps and the use of surveillance technology. The more pressing problem today for both individuals and the law is the uncontrolled dissemination of personal information once an individual has chosen to make a disclosure for a particular purpose. A case in point is the dissemination of information that a victim of venereal disease must furnish to a medical doctor and a public health officer. What will become of such information in either identifiable or anonymous form?

Wasserstrom recognizes that data protection has become most

pressing in recent years. Real problems for privacy arise in areas where individuals lose the kind of control over disclosure that they normally expect to exercise. There are conditions under which none of us can any longer expect to protect our personal privacy. The law must step in to regulate data collection, storage, and dissemination by governments and private organizations. An individual requires the enactment of laws to control what information about him is collected and for what purposes. Any loss of control over information about one's person, not only intimate information, can mean lost privacy and real detriment. Even simple storage of individual data increases the risk of unauthorized access and disclosure. Various forms of data protection, such as the U.S. Privacy Act of 1974, are designed to prevent the misuse of personal data during storage and through various types of linkages. Thus data protection legislation is currently the major societal effort to protect individual privacy.

Some countries, including Sweden, have devised sophisticated technical devices to protect stored data, especially in the hands of government statistical agencies. Strict physical controls are exercised against the risk of unauthorized access. At the same time data in storage are sometimes made anonymous or coded in order to make them unintelligible to an outsider. Wasserstrom raises the issue of the confidentiality of stored arrest and conviction records. The practice of sealing criminal records after the passage of a specified time originated with those concerned for the protection of personal privacy. The crucial element in the collection and dissemination of personal information is the exercise of personal control by an individual through the process of informed consent. Information should be used only for the purposes for which it was collected, unless the respondent has indicated his willingness to allow its reuse for certain purposes, such as in research and statistics. Data protection laws create restrictions on the collection, reuse, and storage of personal information. The alternative is a real loss of the individual's expectation of control over his personal information, and hence a significant invasion of his privacy.

Wasserstrom's general discussion of what privacy means to him illustrates the individualistic character of any personal claim for privacy. He does not care so much about anyone's overhearing his conversation with a travel agent, but he does worry about conversations with his lawyer. This personal account helps the reader locate his or her own place on the spectrum of concern for privacy from Howard Hughes's isolation to the counterculture's openness. Some persons are concerned about certain forms of privacy more than others; the important prerequisite for enjoying privacy is that any individual retains a personal choice to be private in the first instance. To use one of Wasserstrom's cases, privacy in sexual relations has been a standing expectation in Western societies. Sexual intercourse in the great outdoors has a place in Western tradition, but not in the middle of Boston Common in midafternoon. Whatever one's personal preferences, that at least has been the judgment of Massachusetts society since the seventeenth century. In some instances a passionate desire to engage in sexual activity may overcome a reluctance to do so in a public place, thus sacrificing privacy for another goal. Though some primitive societies have apparently not cared very much about sexual privacy, the important point is that an individual should have the freedom to choose a countercultural view of privacy, even if few have done so in recent years. Wasserstrom's observations on the counterculture's relaxed approach to privacy show the degree to which concern for privacy is, and should remain, a matter of personal taste and choice. It is perhaps worth adding that from the perspective of 1978, the counterculture's enthusiasm for total disclosure would appear stillborn. Would any member of today's counterculture love data banks or Big Brother? An assessment of the history of concern for personal privacy in Western societies also does not hold out much hope for the triumph of the counterculture's expansive openness.

Professor Clark's essay, "Privacy, Property, Freedom, and the Family," complements Wasserstrom's effort; Clark is struggling with the problem of achieving a balance of interests affecting privacy. She carries the issue further without ultimately having as many real disagreements with Wasserstrom as she seems to have experienced. Clark's discussion of privacy and freedom, which are hardly identical benefits even in the guise of negative freedom, mainly leads to the essential point that neither is an absolute value. When does an individual's personalized claim of privacy conflict with the needs of society? In practice the search for a balance of interests affecting privacy occurs at the personal, familial, and societal levels. Privacy and freedom are certainly related, as the title of Alan F. Westin's seminal book suggests. But a claim for privacy can be equated with neither negative freedom, freedom itself, nor the idea of being private. Clark gets into some difficulties with such analogies, even though they do help to illuminate the idea of privacy. One should not, as Clark does, "go so far as to say that the right to being alone, or private, is virtually identical with the right to unimpeded activity, or negative freedom." Defining privacy is an absorbing and difficult task. But privacy does not mean simply a "demand for freedom from restraint in at least some area of our lives." Clark is quite correct in asserting that no unlimited claim to either freedom or privacy exists because some private acts can have adverse, unjustifiable consequences for others. A person's claim for privacy has to survive a clash of interests in achieving a balance with other values. A search for solitude, for example, can lead to overwhelming isolation.

Thus Clark's essay is about the limits of privacy. There is no area of unrestricted freedom or of unlimited privacy. But even Wasserstrom does not champion such an absolutist conception of privacy. In a similar vein, it is not the purpose of privacy to serve as a shield for male chauvinism, wife beating, incest, and child abuse. These social problems again illustrate the limits of claims to privacy versus the interests of society's criminal law.

Clark's discussion of privacy and freedom of information is another illustration of the continuing clash of values in an attempt to achieve a balance. The two values are not incompatible despite the difficulties of working out a suitable balance in practice. The American federal government is managing to survive strong statutes for freedom of information and for the protection of personal privacy. The famous Swedish principle of freedom of information is balanced by a secrecy law, which is used to protect the confidentiality of sensitive personal information against detrimental disclosure. In Sweden, the address of a person in a local population register is public information, but an administrative court determined that a former husband did not have any right to obtain the address of his ex-wife because of potential harm to her. Perhaps it is only the experience of living in Canada, where neither the protection of privacy nor freedom of information have any well-developed legal status, which leads one to think that the two values are totally opposed or contradictory in principle. Of course, those opposed to legislation in favor of freedom of information at the federal level in Canada use protection of privacy as a means to delay or dilute such necessary reform. But it may also be illusory to view the advent of freedom of information as redistributing power or equality of opportunity in a society. The major users of the federal freedom of information legislation in the United States appear to be major corporations and their law firms. Even in such countries as the United States and Sweden, the general public knows little about existing laws on privacy and data protection. These are apparently issues for articulate minorities.

Clark's essay illustrates the distinctions between the general concept or claim of personal privacy versus the extremely limited legal right of privacy. Privacy is not simply a legal right or claim. Existing law in Western societies does not protect personal privacy in many areas in which people currently want and often achieve privacy. The legal right of privacy is currently a very narrowly defined legal concept and is likely to remain so everywhere except in the United States, where a majority of the Supreme Court discovered the constitutional right of privacy entrenched in the penumbra of the Bill of Rights. It is fortunate that in many areas of human existence people have been able to enjoy personal privacy on a continuing basis without the intervention of the legal system. But the legal system may ultimately have to protect one's right to make claims and choices for personal privacy. The state may have a duty to uphold my claim or choice to be let alone, so long as all such claims are thought to be in the public interest, or at least harmless, and I have become incapable of protecting these interests myself. In the early twentieth century the state had to intervene to prevent unscrupulous advertisers from using without permission a photograph of a particular person to advertise a commercial product. Computers make possible the uncontrolled collection, storage, and circulation of identifiable individual data; this is another area where most persons require protection from the state. The transfer of data among government departments must be controlled by statute law.

Yet it remains undesirable to transform claims of personal privacy into legal rights, unless it is essential. Maintaining privacy as a primarily nonlegal concept in fact helps to keep regulatory bodies from intruding any more into private lives. It is an achievement for a people to enjoy their choice of privacy on an individual and family basis without the necessity of regular recourse to the law. Families, for example, continue to assert a sphere of intimacy even in the Soviet Union, where privacy has no legal status. Thus individuals must demand their right to privacy at the direct personal level and not rely on the law except in extraordinary circumstances. It is an unfortunate sign of the times when it becomes necessary to legislate against the practice of inquisitive landlords' surveillance devices in the bedrooms of tenants. Thus privacy will remain a somewhat idiosyncratic value, and people, not the law, should normally be free to determine which areas of their lives ought to be free of the scrutiny of others. The result is that citizens of various countries accept varying levels and forms of personal privacy. Residents of English-speaking countries find it difficult to comprehend how Swedes and West Germans can tolerate the existence of sensitive information open to the public in local population registers. But the Swedish public does not view income and age information as sensitive. Residents of the United Kingdom have a very strongly developed sense of privacy, despite very limited legal developments in this area, especially in comparison to those in the United States. Finally, the highly individualistic character of concern for privacy leads Clark into some difficulties when she asserts that privacy is simply an elite value. Public opinion polls in Western countries continue to rate protection of privacy as one of the general public's highest priorities.

Professor Cohen's fascinating essay, "Children and Privacy," is relatively self-explanatory. In particular it develops and applies themes commented on by the two previous authors. Cohen demonstrates the limits of the concept of negative freedom as a useful way of defining privacy. It is also self-evident that a child's claim to privacy can hardly be an absolute one. The limits upon a claim of privacy are particularly acute when placed in the context of the lives of children. As individual families traditionally have had to decide, the question of granting privacy to a child, or assenting to a child's claim of privacy, is a question of balance, not of performance or of negative freedom. A child has as much right to claim privacy as anyone else. How much privacy a child actually obtains is subject to the same competing interests affecting other human beings. The question of a child's right to privacy illustrates again the limited extent of the legal right of privacy. Even in the context of a child's life, lawyers and the legal system can be beneficially kept away from the issue of determining the extent of privacy. There are obvious exceptions, as in the Massachusetts statute Cohen discusses. In this context it is very interesting to reflect on some of Wasserstrom's privacy cases from the point of view of a child's potential claims.

# 13

# Privacy: some arguments and assumptions

## RICHARD A. WASSERSTROM

In this paper I examine some issues involving privacy—issues with which the legal system of the United States has had and continues to have a good deal of concern. What I am interested in is the nature of privacy and the reasons why it might be thought important. The issues I consider have been of particular interest in recent years as changes in technology have made new ways to interfere with privacy possible. For this reason, too, I am primarily concerned with the ways in which government and other powerful institutions can and do interfere with privacy, for it is these institutions that tend to have the sophisticated instruments most at their disposal.

I consider first some distinctions that I think it important to make among different kinds of cases that involve privacy. I then consider in some detail one plausible set of arguments for the value of privacy. These arguments help to explain why the law protects privacy in some of the ways it does and to provide a possible justification for continuing to do so. Some of the arguments are not without their problems, however. And in the final section of the article I raise certain questions about them and indicate the key issues that require additional exploration before any satisfactory justification can be developed.

It is apparent that there are a number of different claims that can be made in the name of privacy. A number—and perhaps all—of them involve the question of the kind and degree of control that a person ought to be able to exercise in respect to knowledge or the disclosure of information about himself or herself. This is not all there is to privacy, but it is surely one central theme.

It is also true that information about oneself is not all of the same type. As a result control over some kinds may be much more important than control over others. For this reason, I want to start by trying to identify some of the different types of information about oneself over which persons might desire to retain control, and I will describe the situations in which this information comes into being. To do this, I will consider four rather ordinary situations and look at the ways they resemble one another and differ from one another.

## I

The cases I have in mind are these.

1. It is midafternoon and I am sitting in a chair resting. As I close my eyes and look inward, I become aware of numerous ideas running through my mind, of various emotions and feelings, and of a variety of bodily sensations—an itch on my scalp, a slight pain in my side, and so on.

2. I am in a closed telephone booth, no one is standing near the booth, and I am talking in a normal voice into the telephone. I have called my travel agent to find out what time there are flights to Chicago so that I can make a reservation for a trip.

3. I am in the bedroom of my home with my wife. We are both undressed, lying on the bed, having sexual intercourse.

4. I am considering hiring a research assistant for the summer. If I wish to, I dial a special number on the telephone and a few days later receive in the mail a computer printout consisting of a profile of the prospective assistant—her age, marital status, arrest record, if any, grades at school, income, as well as a summary of how she has spent her time over the past few years.

The first kind of case is that of the things that are going on within a person's head or body—especially, though, a person's head: his or her mental state. One thing that is significant about my dreams, my conscious thoughts, hopes, fears, and desires is that the most direct, the best, and often the only evidence for you of what they are consists in my deliberately revealing them to you. To be sure, my nonverbal behavior may give an observer a clue as to what is going on in my mind. If, for example, I have a faraway look in my eyes you may infer that I am daydreaming about something and not paying very much attention to you. In addition there is, no doubt, a more intimate and even conceptual connection between observable behavior and certain states of feeling. If I am blushing that may mean that I am embarrassed. If I am talking very fast that may lead you to infer correctly that I am excited or nervous. It is also sometimes the case that I will not know my own thoughts and feelings and that by saying what I think they are, a skilled observer listening to me and watching me as I talk can tell better than can I what is really going on inside my head. This may be one way to describe what can take place during psychotherapy.

But even taking all of these qualifications into account, it still remains the case that the only way to obtain very detailed and accurate information about what I am thinking, fearing, imagining, desiring, or hating and how I am experiencing it is for me to tell you or show you. If I do not, the ideas and feeling remain within me and in some sense, at least, known only to me. Because people cannot read other people's minds, these things about me are known only to me in a way in which other things are not unless I decide to disclose them to you.

What about things that are going on in my body? In some respects the situation is similar to that of my thoughts and in some respects different. There are things that are going on in my body that are like my thoughts, fears, and fantasies. If I have a slight twinge of pain in my left big toe, there is no way for anyone else to know that unless I choose to disclose it. Of course, if the toe is swollen and red and if I grimace whenever I put any weight on it, an observer could doubtless infer correctly that I was experiencing pain there. But in many other cases the only evidence would be my verbal report.

There are other things about my body concerning which this privileged position does not obtain. Even though they are my ribs, I cannot tell very well what they look like; even though it is my blood, I cannot tell with any precision how much alcohol is there. A person looking through a fluoroscope at my ribs or at an x-ray of them can tell far better than I can (just from having them as my ribs or from looking down at my chest) what they look like. A trained technician looking at a sample of my blood in combination with certain chemicals can determine far better than I can (just from it being *my* blood) what the alcohol content is or whether I am anemic.

So there are some facts about my body that I know in a way others logically cannot know them, that can be known to others only if I disclose them by telling what they are. There are other facts about my body that cannot be known by others in the way I know them but that can be inferred from observation of my body and my behavior. And there are still other kinds of facts about my body that I do not know and that can be learned, if at all, only by someone or something outside of myself.

The second kind of case was illustrated by an imagined telephone conversation from a phone booth with my travel agent to make the reservations for a trip. Another case of the same type is this: I am in the dining room of my house, the curtains are drawn, and I am eating dinner with my wife. In both of these cases it is the setting that makes the behavior distinctive and relevant for our purposes. In the example of the reservations over the telephone, the substance of my conversation with my travel agent is within my control if it is the case that no one is in a position to overhear (at my end) what I am saying to him, that no one is listening in along the way, and that only one person, the travel agent, is in a position to hear what I am telling him. It is less within my control, of course, than is information about my mental state, not yet revealed to anyone, because the agent can choose to reveal what I have hold him.

In the second case—that of eating dinner in my dining room— knowledge of what I am eating and how I am eating is in the control of my wife and me if it is correct that no one else is in a position to observe us as we are eating. We might want to describe both of these cases as cases of things being done *in private* (although this is a very weak sense of private)—meaning that they were done in a setting in which there did not appear to be anyone other than the person to whom I was talking or with whom I was eating who was in a position to hear what was being said or to see what was being eaten at the time the behavior was taking place. Both of these are to be contrasted with the third example given earlier.

Instead of eating dinner with my wife in the dining room, we are having sexual intercourse in the bedroom. Or, instead of talking to my travel agent, imagine that I call my lawyer to discuss the terms of my will with her. Both of these things are being done in private in the same sense in which the discussion with the travel agent and the dinner with my wife were private. But these have an additional quality not possessed by the earlier two examples. While I expect that what I tell my lawyer is not being overheard by anyone else while I am telling her, I also reasonably expect that she will keep in confidence what I tell her. The conversation is private in the additional respect that the understanding is that it will not be subsequently disclosed to anyone without my consent. It is a private kind of communication. That is not the case with my phone reservations for Chicago. Absent special or unusual circumstances (for example, telling the agent that I do not want anyone to know when I am going to Chicago), I have no particular interest in retaining control over disclosure of this fact.

Similarly, having intercourse with my wife is private in the additional respect that it is the sort of intimate thing that is not appropriately observed by others or discussed with them—again, absent special or unusual circumstances. In addition to being done in private, it, too, is a private kind of thing. It is in this respect unlike the dinner we had together. There is no expectation on my part that what I ate or how I ate it will not be discussed with others by my wife.

The most obvious and the important connection between the idea of doing something in private and doing a private kind of thing is that we typically do private things only in situations where we reasonably believe that we are doing them in private. That we believe we are doing something in private is often a condition that has to be satisfied before we are willing to disclose an intimate fact about ourselves or to perform an intimate act. I would probably make my airplane reservations even in a crowded travel agency where there were lots of people who could overhear what I was saying. The telephone was a convenient way to make the reservations. But the fact that I was making them in a setting that appeared to be private was not important to me. It did not affect what I disclosed to the agent. Thus, even if I had suspected that my agent's telephone was tapped so that someone unknown to us both overheard our conversation, I would probably have made the reservation. In the case of my conversation with my lawyer, however, it was the belief that the conversation was in a private setting that made me willing to reveal a private kind of information. If someone taped my discussion with my lawyer, he injured me in a way that is distinguishable on this basis alone from the injury, if any, done to me by taping my conversation with the travel agent. That is to say, he got me to do or to reveal something that I would not have done or revealed if they had not hidden his presence from me.

It should be evident, too, that there are important similarities, as well as some differences, between the first and third cases—between my knowledge of my own mental state and my disclosure of intimate or otherwise confidential information to those to whom I choose to disclose it. These can be brought out by considering what it would be like to live in a society whose technology permitted an observer to gain access to the information in question.

## II

Suppose existing technology made it possible for an outsider in some way to look into or monitor another's mind. What, if anything, would be especially disturbing or objectionable about that?

To begin with, there is a real sense in which we have far less control over when we shall have certain thoughts and what their content will be than we have over, for example, to whom we shall reveal them and to what degree. Because our inner thoughts, feelings, and bodily sensations are so largely beyond our control, I think we would feel appreciably more insecure in our social environment than we do at present were it possible for another to "look in" without our consent to see what was going on in our heads.

This is so at least in part because many, although by no means all, of our uncommunicated thoughts and feelings are about very intimate matters. Our fantasies and our fears often concern just those matters that in our culture we would least choose to reveal to anyone else. At a minimum we might suffer great anxiety and feelings of shame were the decisions as to where, when, and to whom we disclose not to be wholly ours. Were access to our thoughts possible in this way, we would see ourselves as creatures who are far more vulnerable than we are now.

In addition, there is a more straightforward worry about accountability for our thoughts and feelings. As I mentioned, they are often not within our control. For all of the reasons that we ought not hold people accountable for behavior not within their control, we would not want the possibility of accountability to extend to uncommunicated thoughts and feelings.

Finally, one rather plausible conception of what it is to be a person carries with it the idea of the existence of a core of thoughts and feelings that are the person's alone. If anyone else could know all that I am thinking or perceive all that I am feeling except in the form I choose to filter and reveal what I am and how I see myself—if anyone could be aware of all this at will—I would cease to have as complete a sense of myself as a distinct and separate person as I have now. A fundamental part of what it is to be an individual is to be an entity that is capable of being exclusively aware of its own thoughts and feelings.

Considerations such as these—and particularly the last one—help us to understand some of the puzzles concerning the privilege against self-incrimination. Because of the significance of exclusive control over our own thoughts and feelings, the privilege against self-incrimination can be seen to rest, ultimately, upon a concern that confessions never be coerced or required by the state. The point of the privilege is not primarily that the state must be induced not to torture individuals in order to extract information from them. Nor is the point even essentially that the topics of confession will necessarily (or even typically) be of the type that we are most unwilling to disclose because of the unfavorable nature of what this would reveal about us. Rather, the fundamental point is that required disclosure of one's thoughts by itself diminishes the concept of individual personhood within the society. For this reason, all immunity statutes that require persons to reveal what they think and believe—provided only that they will not be subsequently prosecuted for what they disclose—are beside the point and properly subject to criticism. For this reason, too, cases that permit the taking of a blood sample (to determine alcohol content) from an unconscious or unwilling person—despite the existence of the privilege—are also defensible. Since a person is not in a privileged position in respect to the alcohol content of his or her own blood, the claim to exclusivity in respect to knowledge of this fact is not particularly persuasive.

In a society in which intrusion into the domain of one's uncommunicated thoughts and feelings was not possible, but in which communications between persons about private things could be intercepted, some of the problems would remain the same. To begin with, because of our social attitudes toward the disclosure of intimate facts and behavior, most of us would be extremely pained were we to learn that these had become known to persons other than those to whom we chose to disclose them. The pain can come about in several different ways. If I do something private with somebody and I believe that we are doing it in private, I may very well be hurt or embarrassed if I learn subsequently that we were observed but did not know it. Thus if I learn after the fact that someone had used a special kind of telescope to observe my wife and me while we were having intercourse, the knowledge that we were observed will cause us distress both because our expectations of privacy were incorrect and because we do not like the idea that we were observed during this kind of intimate act. People have the right to have the world be what it appears to be precisely in those cases in which they regard privacy as essential to the diminution of their own vulnerability.

Reasoning such as this lies behind, I think, a case that arose some years ago in California. A department store had complained to the police that homosexuals were using its men's room as a meeting place. The police responded by drilling a small hole in the ceiling over the enclosed stalls. A policeman then stationed himself on the floor above and peered down through the hole observing the persons using the stall for eliminatory purposes. Eventually the policeman discovered and apprehended two homosexuals who used the stall as a place to engage in forbidden sexual behavior. The California Supreme Court held the observations of the policeman to have been the result of an illegal search and ordered the conviction reversed. What made the search illegal, I believe, was that it occurred in the course of this practice, which deceived all of the persons who used the stall and who believed that they were doing in private something that was socially regarded as a private kind of thing. They were entitled, especially for this kind of activity, both to be free from observation and to have their expectations of privacy honored by the state.

There is an additional reason why the observation of certain sorts of activity is objectionable. That is because the kind of spontaneity and openness that is essential to them disappears with the presence of an observer. To see that this is so, consider a different case. Suppose I know in advance that we will be observed during intercourse. Here there is no problem of defeated reasonable expectations. But there may be injury nonetheless. For one thing, I may be unwilling or unable to communicate an intimate fact or engage in intimate behavior in the presence of an observer. In this sense I will be quite directly prevented from going forward. In addition, even if I do go ahead, the character of the experience may very well be altered. Knowing that someone is watching or listening may render what would have been an enjoyable experience unenjoyable. Or, having someone watch or listen may so alter the character of the relationship that it is simply not the same kind of relationship it was before. The presence of the observer may make spontaneity impossible. Aware of the observer, I am engaged in part in viewing or imagining what is going on from his or her perspective. I thus cannot lose myself as completely in the activity.

Suppose, to take still a third case, I do not know whether I am being observed or overheard, but I reasonably believe that no matter what the appearances, it is possible that I am being observed or overheard. I think it quite likely that the anxiety produced by not knowing whether one is doing an intimate act in private is often more painful and more destructive than the certain knowledge that one is being observed or overheard, despite all precautions. It is possible, for example, that one could adjust more easily and successfully in a world where one could never do things in private than one could in a world where there was always a rational likelihood that one was being deceived about the ostensible privacy in which one was acting. This is so because the worry about whether an observer was present might interfere more with the possibility of spontaneity than would the knowledge that the observer was there. If I am correct, then one of the inevitable consequences of living in a society in which sophisticated spying devices are known to exist and to be used is that it does make more rational the belief that one may be being observed or overheard no matter what the appearances. And this in turn makes engagement more difficult.

There is still an additional reason why control over intimate facts and behavior might be of appreciable importance to individuals: our social universe would be altered in fundamental and deleterious ways were that control to be surrendered or lost. This is so because one way in which we mark off and distinguish certain interpersonal relationships from other ones is in terms of the kind of intimate information and behavior that we are willing to share with other persons. One way in which we make someone a friend rather than an acquaintance is by revealing things about ourselves to that person that we do not reveal to the world at large. On this view some degree of privacy is a logically necessary condition for the existence of many of our most meaningful social relationships.

## III

The fourth kind of case that I want to consider is different from the previous three. It is suggested by the example I gave earlier of all of the information that might be made routinely available to me concerning possible appointees to the job of teaching assistant. It concerns the consequences of possessing the technological capability to store an enormous amount of information about each of the individual members of a society in such a way that the information can be retrieved and presented in a rapid, efficient, and relatively inexpensive fashion. This topic—the character, uses, and dangers of data banks—is one that has received a lot of attention in recent years. I think the worries are legitimate and that the reasons for concern have been too narrowly focused.

Consider a society in which the kinds of data collected about an individual are not very different from the kinds and quantity already collected in some fashion or other in our own society. It is surprising what a large number of interactions are deemed sufficiently important to record in some way. Thus, there are, for example, records of the traffic accidents I have been in, the applications I have made for life insurance, the purchases that I have made with my Mastercharge card, the COD packages I have signed for, the schools my children are enrolled in, the telephone numbers that have been called from my telephone, and so on. Now suppose that all of this information, which is presently recorded in some written fashion, were to be stored in some way so that it could be extracted on demand. What would result?

It is apparent that at least two different kinds of pictures of me would emerge. First, some sort of a qualitative picture of the kind of person I am would emerge. A whole lot of nontemporal facts would be made available—what kind of driver I am, how many children I have, what sorts of purchases I have made, how often my telephone is used, how many times I have been arrested and for what offenses, what diseases I have had, how much life insurance I have, and so on.

Second, it would also be possible to reconstruct a rough, temporal picture of how I had been living and what I had been doing with my time. Thus, there might be evidence that I visited two or three stores in a day and made purchases, that I cashed a check at the bank (and hence was there between the hours of 10 A.M. and 3 P.M.), that I ate lunch at a particular restaurant (and hence was probably there between noon and 2 P.M.), and so on. There might well be whole days for which there were no entries, and there might be many days for which the entries would give a very sketchy and incomplete picture of how I was spending my time. Still, it would be a picture that is fantastically more detailed, accurate, and complete than the one I could supply from my own memory or from my own memory as it is augmented by that of my friends. I would have to spend a substantial amount of time each day writing in my diary in order to begin to produce as complete and accurate a picture as the one that might be rendered by the storage and retrieval system I am envisaging—and even then I am doubtful that my own diary would be as accurate or as complete, unless I made it one of my major life tasks to keep accurate and detailed records for myself of everything that I did.

If we ask whether there would be anything troublesome about living in such a society, the first thing to recognize is that there are several different things that might be objectionable. First, such a scheme might make communications that were about intimate kinds of things less confidential. In order to receive welfare, life insurance, or psychiatric counseling, I may be required to supply information of a personal or confidential nature. If so, I reasonably expect that the material revealed will be known only to the recipient.

If, however, the information is stored in a data bank, it now becomes possible for the information to be disclosed to persons other than those to whom disclosure was intended. Even if access to the data is controlled so as to avoid the risks of improper access, storage of the confidential information in the data bank necessarily makes the information less confidential that it was before it was so stored.

Second, information that does not concern intimate things can get distorted in one way or another through storage. The clearest contemporary case of this kind of information is a person's arrest record. The fact that someone has been arrested is not, I think, the kind of fact that the arrestee can insist ought to be kept secret. But he or she can legitimately make two other demands about it. The person can insist that incorrect inferences not be drawn from the information; that is, the person can legitimately point out that many individuals who are arrested are never prosecuted for the alleged offense nor are they guilty of the offense for which they were arrested. He or she can, therefore, quite appropriately complain about any practice that routinely and without more being known denies employment to persons with arrest records. And if such a practice exists, then a person can legitimately complain about the increased dissemination and availability of arrest records just because of the systematic misuse of that information. The storage of arrest records in a data bank becomes objectionable not because the arrest record is intrinsically private but because the information is so regularly misused that the unavailability of the information is less of an evil than its general availability.

This does not end the matter, although this is where the discussion of data banks usually ends. Let us suppose that the information is appropriately derogatory in respect to the individual. Suppose that it is a record of arrest and conviction in circumstances that in no way suggest that the conviction was unfairly or improperly obtained. Does the individual have any sort of a claim that information of this sort not be put into the data bank? One might, of course, complain on the grounds that there was a practice of putting too much weight on the conviction. Here the argument would be similar to that just discussed. In addition, though, it might also be maintained that there are important gains that come from living in a society in which certain kinds of derogatory information about an individual are permitted to disappear from view after a certain amount of time. What is involved is the creation of a kind of social environment that holds out to the members of the society the possibility of self-renewal and change that is often dependent upon the individual's belief that a fresh start is in fact an option that is still open. A society that is concerned to encourage persons to believe in the possibility of genuine individual redemption and that is concerned not to make the process of redemption unduly onerous or interminable might, therefore, actively discourage the development of institutions that impose permanent marks of disapprobation upon any of the individuals in the society. One of the things that I think was wrong with Hester Prynne's "A" was that it was an unremovable stain impressed upon her body. The storage of information about convictions in a data bank is simply a more contemporary method of affixing the indelible brand.

In addition, and related to some of the points I made earlier, there are independent worries about the storage of vast quantities of ostensibly innocuous material about the individual in the data bank. Suppose nothing intrinsically private is stored in the data bank; suppose nothing potentially or improperly derogatory is included; and suppose what does get stored is an enormous quantity of information about the individual—information about the person and the public, largely commercial, transactions that were entered into. There are many useful, efficient uses to which such a data bank might be put. Can there be any serious objections?

One thing is apparent. With such a data bank it would be possible to reconstruct a person's movements and activities more accurately and completely than the individual—or any group of individuals—could do simply from memory. As I have indicated, there would still be gaps in the picture. No one would be able to tell in detail what the individual had been doing a lot of the time, but the sketch would be a surprisingly rich and comprehensive one that is exceeded in detail in our society only by the keeping of a careful, thorough personal diary or by having someone under the surveillance of a corps of private detectives.

What distinguishes this scheme is the fact that it would make it possible to render an account of the movements and habits of every member of the society and in so doing it might transform the society in several notable respects.

In part what is involved is the fact that every transaction in which one engages would now take on additional significance. In such a society one would be both buying a tank of gas and leaving a part of a systematic record of where one was on that particular date. One would not just be applying for life insurance; one would also be recording in a permanent way one's health on that date and a variety of other facts about oneself. No matter how innocent one's intentions and actions at any given moment, I think that an inevitable consequence of such a practice of data collection would be that persons would think more carefully before they did things that would become part of the record. Life would to this degree become less spontaneous and more measured.

More significant are the consequences of such a practice upon attitudes toward privacy in the society. If it became routine to record and have readily accessible vast quantities of information about every individual, we might come to hold the belief that the detailed inspection of any individual's behavior is a perfectly appropriate societal undertaking. We might tend to take less seriously than we do at present the idea that there are occasions upon which an individual can plausibly claim to be left alone and unobserved. We might in addition become so used to being objects of public scrutiny that we would cease to deem privacy important in any of our social relationships. As observers we might become insensitive to the legitimate claims of an individual to a sphere of life in which the individual is at present autonomous and around which he or she can erect whatever shield is wished. As the subjects of continual observation we might become forgetful of the degree to which many of the most important relationships within which we now enter depend for their existence upon the possibility of privacy.

On the other hand, if we do continue to have a high regard for privacy, both because of what it permits us to be as individuals and because of the kinds of relationships and activities it makes possible and promotes, the maintenance of a scheme of systematic data collection would necessarily get in the way. This is so for the same reason discussed earlier. Much of the value and significance of being able to do intimate things in private is impaired whenever there is a serious lack of confidence about the privacy of the situation. No one could rationally believe that the establishment of data banks—no matter how pure the motives of those who maintain and have access to them—is calculated to enhance the confidentiality of much that is now known about each one of us. And even if only apparently innocuous material is to be stored, we could never be sure that it all was as innocuous as it seemed at the time. It is very likely, therefore, that we would go through life alert to these new, indelible consequences of everyday interactions and transactions. Just as our lives would be different from what they are now if we believed that every telephone conversation was being overheard, so our lives would be similarly affected if we believed that every transaction and application was being stored. In both cases we would go through life encumbered by a wariness and deliberateness that would make it less easy to live what we take to be the life of a free person.

## IV

The foregoing constitute, I believe, a connected set of arguments for the distinctive value of privacy. While I find them persuasive, I also believe that some of them are persuasive only within the context of certain fundamental assumptions and presuppositions. And these assumptions and these presuppositions seem to be a good deal more problematic than is often supposed. What remains to be done, therefore, is to try to make them explicit so that they can then be subjected to analysis and assessment. One way to do this is to ask whether there is an alternative perspective through which a number of these issues might be considered. I believe that there is. I call it the perspective of the counterculture because it captures at least some of the significant ingredients of that point of view or way of life. In calling this alternative view the perspective of the counterculture, I do not mean to be explicating a view that was in fact held by any person or group. However, this view does provide a rationale for a number of the practices and ideals of one strain of the counterculture movement in the United States in the 1960s.

I have argued for the importance of reposing control over the disclosure or observation of intimate facts with the actor. One argument for doing so was that intimate facts about oneself—one's fears, fantasies, jealousies, and desires—are often embarrassing if disclosed to others than those to whom we choose to disclose them. Similarly there are acts of various sorts that cause us pain or are rendered unenjoyable unless they are done alone or in the company only of those we choose to have with us.

This is a significant feature of our culture—or at least of the culture in which I grew up. What I am less sure about is the question of whether it is necessarily a desirable feature of a culture. Indeed disagreement about just this issue seems to me to be one of the major sources of tension between the counterculture and the dominant older culture of my country. The disagreement concerns both a general theory of interpersonal relationships and a view about the significance of intimate thoughts and actions. The alternative view goes something like this.

We have made ourselves vulnerable—or at least far more vulnerable than we need be—by accepting the notion that there are thoughts and actions concerning which we ought to feel ashamed or embarrassed. When we realize that everyone has fantasies, desires, worries about all sorts of supposedly terrible, wicked, and shameful things, we ought to see that they really are not things to be ashamed of at all. We regard ourselves as vulnerable because in part we think we are different, if not unique. We have sexual feelings toward our parents, and no one else has ever had such wicked feelings. But if everyone does, then the fact that others know of this fantasy is less threatening. One is less vulnerable to their disapproval and contempt.

We have made ourselves excessively vulnerable, so this alternative point of view continues, because we have accepted the idea that many things are shameful unless done in private. And there is no reason to accept that convention. Of course we are embarrassed if others watch us having sexual intercourse—just as we are embarrassed if others see us unclothed. But that is because the culture has taught us to have these attitudes and not because they are intrinsically fitting. Indeed our culture would be healthier and happier if we diminished substantially the kinds of actions that we now feel comfortable doing only in private, or the kind of thoughts we now feel comfortable disclosing only to those with whom we have special relationships. This is so for at least three reasons. In the first place, there is simply no good reason why privacy is essential to these things. Sexual intercourse could be just as pleasurable in public (if we grew up unashamed) as is eating a good dinner in a good restaurant. Sexual intercourse is better in private only because society has told us so.

In the second place, it is clear that a change in our attitudes will make us more secure and at ease in the world. If we would be as indifferent to whether we are being watched when we have intercourse as we are to when we eat a meal, then we cannot be injured by the fact that we know others are watching us, and we cannot be injured nearly as much by even unknown observations.

In the third place, interpersonal relationships will in fact be better if there is less of a concern for privacy. After all, forthrightness, honesty, and candor are, for the most part, virtues, while hypocrisy and deceit are not. Yet this emphasis upon the maintenance of a private side to life tends to encourage hypocritical and deceitful ways of behavior. Individuals see themselves as leading dual lives—public ones and private ones. They present one view of themselves to the public—to casual friends, acquaintances, and strangers—and a different view of themselves to themselves and a few intimate associates. This way of living is hypocritical because it is, in essence, a life devoted to camouflaging the real, private self from public scrutiny. It is a dualistic, unintegrated life that renders the individuals who live it needlessly vulnerable, shame ridden, and lacking in a clear sense of self. It is to be contrasted with the more open, less guarded life of the person who has so little to fear from disclosures of self because he or she has nothing that requires hiding.

I think that this is an alternative view that deserves to be taken seriously. Any attempt to do so, moreover, should begin by considering more precisely the respects in which it departs from the more conventional view of the role of privacy maintained in the body of this essay, and the respects in which it does not. I have in mind three issues in particular that must be examined in detail before an intelligent decision can be made. The first is the question of the value that the counterculture ideal attaches to those characteristics of spontaneity and individuality that play such an important role in the more traditional view as I have described it. On at least one interpretation both views prize spontaneity and individuality equally highly, with the counterculture seeing openness in interpersonal relationships as a better way of achieving just those ends. On another interpretation, however, autonomy, spontaneity, and individuality are replaced as values by the satisfactions that attend the recognition of the likeness of all human experience and the sameness that characterizes all interpersonal relationships. Which way of living gives one more options concerning the kind of life that one will fashion for oneself is one of the central issues to be settled.

Still another issue that would have to be explored is the question of what would be gained and what would be lost in respect to the character of interpersonal relationships. One of the main arguments for the conventional view put forward earlier is that the sharing of one's intimate thoughts and behavior is one of the primary media through which close, meaningful interpersonal relationships are created, nourished, and confirmed. One thing that goes to define a relationship of close friendship is that the friends are willing to share truths about themselves with each other that they are unprepared to reveal to the world at large. One thing that helps to define and sustain a sexual love relationship is the willingness of the parties to share sexual intimacies with each other that they are unprepared to share with the world at large. If this makes sense, either as a conceptual or as an empirical truth, then perhaps acceptance of the counterculture ideal would mean that these kinds of relationships were either no longer possible or less likely. Or perhaps the conventional view is equally unsatisfactory here, too. Perhaps friendship and love both can and ought to depend upon some less proprietary, commercial conception of the exchange of commodities. Perhaps this view of intimate interpersonal relationships is as badly in need of alteration as is the attendant conception of the self.

Finally, we would want to examine more closely some other features of the counterculture ideal. Even if we no longer thought it important to mark off and distinguish our close friends from strangers (or even if we could still do that, but in some other way), might not the counterculture ideal of openness and honesty in all interpersonal relationships make ordinary social interaction vastly more complex and time-consuming than it now is—so much so, in fact, that these interactions, rather than the other tasks of living, would become the focus of our waking hours?

These are among the central issues that require continued exploration. They are certainly among the issues that the fully developed theory of privacy, its value and its place within the law, must confront and not settle by way of assumption and presupposition.

# 14

# Privacy, property, freedom, and the family

**LORENNE M. G. CLARK**

The issue of privacy and the law is vastly complicated, both in theory and in practice. Almost as complicated is the relationship of this problem to some issues in philosophy. Nothing can usefully be said, much less done, until some of these complications are sorted out. For these reasons I think it necessary to attempt at least a sketch of a framework in which these issues should be discussed and analyzed. Thus, it is my intention to divide my article into three parts. In the first part I want to attempt such a schema and in the second and third to discuss some of the major issues within that framework.

## I

Discussions as to whether there ought to be a legally entrenched right to privacy seem to me to be virtually identical to the disputes in philosophy as to whether there should be an area of one's life in which one has an unlimited right to freedom.[1] Putting the problem this way raises the inevitable problem as to the nature and kinds of freedom individual citizens have or ought to have. It also permits us to draw parallels between concepts of privacy and concepts of freedom and to work out some of the relationships between them. I want to develop the view that privacy is to the law what freedom is to political philosophy and to pursue the parallels as far as they go.

We must acknowledge from the outset that the interest we have in privacy is twofold. It is an interest, first, in the sense that we place a moral value on it, articulating our demand for freedom from restraint in at least some areas of our lives. Clearly whether this should remain an interest that we wish our society and our legal system to protect is one of the major issues to be resolved, and it is this aspect of the issue that is the sole concern of Professor Wasserstrom. Certainly the definitions of "privacy" offered in the courts and discussed in the literature bear a strong resemblance to the definition of freedom that goes under the designation "negative freedom." Wasserstrom's paper is among the best examples I can think of to illustrate the point. He treats privacy as a necessary condition of doing things, of enjoying certain areas of one's life free from the scrutiny and arbitrary invasion of others. He remarks that in living in a data-bank society, "We would go through life encumbered by a wariness and deliberateness that would make it less easy to live what we take to be the life of a free person," and clearly he means here a person who is free of legal restraints on his behavior in certain key areas, those of interpersonal relationships in particular but not exclusively. Negative freedom is the freedom to do what I want, to be unrestricted in the pursuit of my interests as I see them.

One could go so far as to say that the right to being let alone, or private, is virtually identical with the right to unimpeded activity, or negative freedom. If not identical, the one certainly entails the other, since I shall not be able to do what I want if I am not let alone by others. In short, one must be free of the unrestrained scrutiny and arbitrary invasion of others if one is to be able to pursue one's own interests: one must be private in order to be free and be free in order to be private. But if this is so, then surely the right to privacy ought to be subject to at least the same restrictions as the right to negative freedom.

Within the framework of classical liberalism, this means at least that one ought to be entitled only to as much privacy as does not interfere with a like privacy of others. I am no more entitled to a privacy with respect to property that necessitates that others should have no privacy at all than I am entitled to a freedom that necessitates enslaving others. Freedom in this sense is clearly a defeasible concept insofar as it relates to practical actions. I am prima facie entitled to do as I please unless there are defeating conditions that would make the operation of my right incompatible with the operation of like rights for others. Thus, the reasons for denying my freedom in certain circumstances are directly connected with the same principles giving rise to the right in the first place, namely, that each person is entitled to the same degree of liberty as every other. Hence, incursions against my liberty are justified if and only if the exercise of my right would render inoperable the similar rights of others. Conversely I am justified in doing whatever does not substantially restrict the operation of the similar rights of others. And so for privacy. Privacy, too, is a defeasible concept; I am prima facie entitled to privacy unless the similar right of others would be adversely affected as a consequence of my exercising the right. Thus, the point to be established here is that there is no basis for arguing that one has an unlimited right to either freedom or privacy. Each person is entitled to as much freedom and/or privacy as is compatible with like rights for others.

Also the alleged right to privacy and the alleged right to freedom are alike in that both are clearly privileges rather than claims, at least insofar as they are stated in this unrestricted fashion. The state does not have a duty to uphold my demand to do what I want or to be let alone. At most, it permits me to do what I am not prohibited from doing. I am thus free in the negative sense to the extent that the law imposes neither legal duties nor legal restraints upon me, and private to the extent that the law imposes neither legal duties of disclosure nor legal restraints as to private transactions.

The policy questions arise, of course, at precisely this juncture. Under what conditions is the state justified in imposing such duties and restraints upon me? The answer is, When the absence of such duties and restraints would substantially impair the ability of others to exercise rights of a similar sort. Thus, the effective exercise of the privileges of some can in some circumstances be realized only by limiting the similar privileges of others. This is to say that an equal distribution of effective or exercisable rights can sometimes be achieved only by converting privileges into claims, that is, by imposing duties on some, thereby giving rise to correlative claims on the part of others.[2] Thus, the privileges of all, which can in particular de facto situations be effectively exercised only by some, must give way to the mutual acquisition of duties, thus giving rise to a claim on the part of each. The real problem about privacy is to decide whether, and for what reason or reasons, we ought to extinguish legally the privilege each has to privacy in favor of equally distributed claims and their correlative duties. Should others, any others, be legally prohibited from finding out certain things about anyone else? To ask that question is to ask a fundamental question about negative freedom: should there be any areas of one's life, and if so which ones, about which others are duty-bound not to interfere? That is the question I will try to answer in the second part of my article and within which I shall discuss Wasserstrom's article because that is basically the question, and the only question, he is asking.

Related to these issues, but cutting across them to some extent, is a further problem. Since the entrenchment of a claim-right to privacy would effectively limit access to information, and since access to information is necessary to facilitate our economic and social interests, some argue that there ought not to be any entrenched right to privacy since this would conflict with the equal right of all to access to information. Thus, it is held, an individual claim-right to privacy is incompatible with a public right to knowledge. Clearly, there is something to this argument, which must be considered in any adequate treatment of the issue. The task is to work out some of the relationships between this problem and those I have already outlined. This can be done by giving a careful account of the extent to which our problems about privacy arise from conceiving of it as a form of negative freedom and from failing to see that limitations of the privilege to privacy that some persons already have is necessary to promote equal access to information.

Privacy is an interest in the sense that it is a moral value that (at least up to now) we have wanted our legal system to protect because it preserves an area of negative freedom many believe to be necessary to the notion of respect for the autonomy of the individual. However, privacy is also clearly an interest in an economic and social sense as well, and it is this aspect of the problem that is related to the issue of a public right to knowledge. This is not an issue discussed by Wasserstrom but is one that must be dealt with.

It is becoming obvious to a great many people that information is rapidly becoming the basis of power.[3] As larger numbers of people begin to perceive information as power, access to information is being perceived as a necessary condition of self-determination. As such, access to information is rapidly replacing property as a precondition of power. Thus, people are beginning to demand access to information as a property right. In this technological age power is shifting from the owners of land to the people who have access to advanced information systems and who have the political power to manipulate information bureaucracies to their own advantage. Given that this is true, equality of opportunity surely demands that there should be equal access to the information necessary to achieve the good life as it is understood in liberal democratic societies.

Obviously, were access to information unnecessary to the promotion of individual economic interests, there would be no need to ensure its availability to the public. Just because it is the new basis of power and is replacing property as the central value around which the legal system rotates, it is necessary to afford it the protection it needs in order to articulate and protect those further values that it serves. This is to argue essentially that the end of equal opportunity for power requires equal access to information as a means to that end and that since an individual claim-right to privacy would frustrate that end, there should be no entrenched claim-right to privacy.

This argument seems to neglect the lessons taught us by an analysis of how property has functioned in the development of liberal democracies. In common law cultures, privacy has been indelibly linked with property. With advances in industrialization, the ownership of property became the necessary condition of familial privacy. This is made clear by even a superficial examination of the history of privacy, in which privacy was conceived spatially and evolved doctrinally through the laws of trespass and nuisance. Thus, privacy was and is a privilege-right historically and practically linked with the ownership of property. The ability to exercise this privilege effectively—that is, the ability to be private—is one of the incidents of ownership. As such, it became a commodity purchased with property or inherited through class standing. This historical legacy has profoundly influenced the present-day social status of privacy. It is a commodity rewarded to those who enjoy high social status within our society, top management in industry and government, and professional elites, such as doctors, lawyers, and university professors. It is awarded along with high social rank. The assumption has been that such persons of education and wealth were responsible individuals, as concerned with the public good as with the advancement of their own interests. The public, or at least everyone else, has been denied knowledge of the alleged private actions and affairs of such persons and of the working habits of these elites. By contrast, workers, minor officials, and others less well placed in the social structure have always been under much greater surveillance, unable to establish limits on managerial and governmental intrusion into their habits and private lives. Property has thus been a necessary condition of privacy and has functioned to create and foster an elite, thus frustrating the alleged right of equal opportunity to occupy positions of political power.

If access to information is genuinely evolving as the "new property" (that is, if property is now beginning to be construed as access to information—and that, I believe, is true), what reason do we have for believing that this will not also evolve as a necessary condition for privacy and hence continue to foster an elite and the concentration of power in the hands of that elite? Those with privacy were, and are, in a privileged position with respect to the gaining of those social goods we believed to be desirable. In the past, property was the basis for this privacy and now, or certainly in the near future, access to information will be the basis for it. The point is, that since individuals do not start out from positions of equality, it is necessary to limit the privacy some already have that allows them to perpetuate an elite that already has concentrated power in its own hands. It is therefore necessary to accord a claim-right to privacy to those who cannot now exercise their privilege in order to prevent them from falling further behind in their ability to acquire and use information to their own economic and social advantage and to prevent others from acquiring information about their work and private lives which is presently used by those in power to entrench their power further. Thus, the framework within which the issue of privacy ought to be discussed involves basically two questions. First, is the moral interest we have in privacy one that ought to be preserved and, indeed, strengthened? Second, if the economic interest we have in privacy necessitates the granting of a claim-right to individual privacy, which then places each under a duty not to extract certain kinds of information from others, what are the areas within which each individual should be thus protected? It is at this point that the two sets of problems overlap, for the problem for negative freedom has been and remains what the areas are within which one should be free of the restraints and/or impositions of others. One might be tempted to presume, or perhaps simply to hope, that the areas within which we have a moral interest in privacy might also be the ones that should be legally off-limits in order to promote equality of opportunity, but it would be premature at this point to come to that conclusion. However, I shall now turn my attention to the first question and to answering Wasserstrom.

## II

Freedom does not presuppose a distinction between the parts of one's life, a private as opposed to a public sphere, though recent disputes on the nature and justified extent of one's freedom have centered around this distinction. The classical position remains that there must be an irreducible part of one's life that is essentially private and about which the law has no business either imposing duties or restraints. The problem has always been to try to define what ought to be included within that area, for the point of drawing the line is to say that things behind that line are inviolate from the scrutiny of anyone else, at least insofar as that scrutiny gives rise to legal consequences. If the proponents of this view of freedom could give such a definition, then we would also have generated a domain, or at least a minimum or partial domain, for the concept of privacy, namely, an area immune from the scrutiny of the law. If there were an area in which we agreed that people should be entitled to do exactly as they please, then we would also have generated a right to privacy, namely, the right to do those sorts of things immune from deleterious consequences.

Wasserstrom identifies several areas over which "persons might desire to retain control." These include what he terms the "intrinsically private"—my thoughts and feelings and those facts about my body "that I know in a way others logically cannot know them, that can be known by others only if I disclose them by telling what they are." These also include facts about my body that are opaque to me, such as the state of my lungs, which "can be learned . . . only by someone or something outside of myself." First of all, I would like to challenge the category of the "intrinsically private." Whether there are any things intrinsically, or essentially, private in the way that Wasserstrom wants to hold is surely arguable. Indeed, in entertaining the possibility that our thoughts could be monitored, he is surely denying that anything can be known to be intrinsically private. But in any case, if some version of the identity theory turns out to be true, then the intrinsically private does not exist. While I certainly do not intend to argue for or against that metaphysical thesis here, I certainly would not want to rest a case for privacy on its nonexistence. The identity thesis notwithstanding, the possibility of the thought-police seems to me to draw ever closer, and if we feel we have any good reasons for prohibiting incursions of this kind, I would not feel on any very safe ground resting them on the terrain of the intrinsically private.

This approach misses the issue even as Wasserstrom sets it up. It does not seem obvious that the reasons why we would not want our thoughts monitored has anything to do with the general principle that we ought not to hold people accountable for what is not within their control. He seems to think of the mind and its addenda as a sort of all-night movie of a rather unsavory sort, going on endlessly, reel after reel. Surely our reason for not wanting to be held responsible for our thoughts alone is the fact that we are not yet convinced that there is an unavoidable, inevitable connection between thought and action. Again we seem to be into shifty metaphysical quicksand. Surely the point here has to be that at least until someone commits a prohibited *actus*, we feel it unjustified to hold him accountable purely for his thoughts. Perhaps that does ultimately rest on some presumption about free will, but it seems to me that at least until we can establish that there is some sort of ironclad necessity regarding the relation of thought and action, we ought to give people the benefit of a reasonable doubt.

On the other hand, were it to turn out that there is such a connection, what would be wrong with monitoring people's thoughts? If it is wrong at all, it is because we believe that some of the things people do have adverse effects on others, and hence if we knew that action followed thought with the speed of lightning we would surely be justified in monitoring some thoughts. The point here is that not even that would license monitoring all thoughts. The reasons why we ought to limit thoughts or actions must have to do with the consequences they have for others, and once that is seen to be the relevant reason for justifying interference, then it does not matter whether there is any strong connection between thought and action. The metaphysical realities are irrelevant to the moral issues. If the moral and/or legal guidelines are laid down, then the metaphysical outcome does not matter. Indeed, there are already many instances in which we do hold persons accountable for mere thoughts. Priests do it all the time; so do psychiatrists charged with the responsibility of deciding whether those adjudged criminally insane can be safely released from custody; parole boards make much the same kind of decision.

But there is another important issue here too. Wasserstrom argues that our concept of personhood is bound up with our belief in the intrinsic privateness of our thoughts, and hence that any coerced disclosure of one's thoughts shows a disrespect for and somehow diminishes the concept of individual personhood. It is on the basis of this reasoning that he holds that it is unjustifiable ever to compel disclosure of our thoughts and beliefs but justified to require the taking of a blood sample to determine alcohol content. Since the former is intrinsically private, it is wrong; since the latter is not, it is right. Clearly we could still have the concept of a person as an entity having some things intrinsically private about it and nonetheless fail to have respect for the particular persons who instantiate the concept. Compulsory disclosure of anything does nothing to destroy the concept of personhood, though some coerced disclosures equally clearly could be said to display a disrespect for persons.

This argument seems to have the cart before the horse. Our desire to treat persons as deserving of respect, as being worthy of being allowed the benefit of the doubt, and even occasionally the freedom of their consciences may be part of what leads us to the view that persons are entities with some things about them that are deeply private. But again, it seems that it is our moral judgment to treat people as deserving of respect that leads to our attributing to them areas in which they will be left to their own discretion rather than that it is our assumption as to their metaphysical status which leads to our treating them as worthy of respect. After all, we could have a concept of personhood that in no way depended on any such metaphysical assumption; indeed we could have a concept of personhood such that nothing was held to be private in principal and still treat persons as worthy of respect and as deserving discretion with respect to some areas of their lives. But it seems that this confusion lies at the basis of the blood sample example. If there is nothing intrinsically private, then any kind of interference will be justified. Again, if we want to prevent interference of certain sorts, whether we do so ought to depend on the moral reasons we advance and not on the kinds of things being interfered with. The decision as to what ought to be legally coercible must be made independently of judgments as to the metaphysical nature of the things. It seems to me that compulsory blood testing is justified when the person has been found to be driving in an unsafe manner since that it likely to lead the injury to others, not because it just happens to be something that I cannot know about directly. And the same reasons justify at least some compelled disclosures of our thoughts and feelings.

But now I want to consider Wasserstrom's distinction between doing something in private and doing a private kind of thing. Presumably these, too, are areas in which we wish to retain control. Wasserstrom contends that there is a connection such that one typically does private kinds of things only in private. The converse, however, does not hold; not everything done in private is a private kind of thing. Thus he says, "That we believe we are doing something in private is often a condition that has to be satisfied before we are willing to disclose an intimate fact about ourselves or to perform an intimate act." This seems to me to be an argument designed to show that doing something in private is a necessary condition of doing a private kind of thing. Just what makes something private is not clear. It seems to be that it is the sort of thing that, when done in private, leads to the expectation that it will not subsequently be disclosed to anyone else without one's consent. However, Wasserstrom's account of the relation between these things also suggests that doing something with the understanding that it will not be disclosed to others without consent is what is meant by doing something in private. It is unclear whether Wasserstrom wants to claim that private kinds of things are just the sorts of things that give rise to such expectations, and whether being done in private, regardless of the nature of the thing, is what gives rise to such expectations or whether it is the doing of private kinds of things in private that gives rise to such expectations. But that aside, what right does anyone have to such expectations?

Some further distinctions seem to be necessary. Certainly there must be different classes of private kinds of things. First, there are activities that just happen to be done in private, at least in the sense that they are typically done out of the sight or earshot of others. At least some of the things that might be members of this class do not seem to bear any relation to the notion that the doing of them creates an expectation of nondisclosure. Sleeping and going to the toilet seem to me to be these sorts of things. Typically we do these things in some sense privately, but certainly we do not care whether it is disclosed to others that we are doing them. Indeed it is often necessary to disclose this in order to prevent one's activity from being disturbed. Second, there are things typically done out of the sight or earshot of others, which may also be done with the expectation of nondisclosure but where such nondisclosure could in no sense be said to be a duty of the other participant. Sexual intercourse, whether with one's spouse or not, seems a plausible candidate for this class. Sexual intimacy usually is engaged in in the spatially private sense, and it frequently is done with the expectation that it will not be bandied about in public. But surely it could not be claimed that it is in any sense an intrinsically private kind of thing. That it is is the result of social conditioning. While Wasserstrom seems to be wanting to claim some metaphysical status for things of this kind, it is a claim he must give up, indeed, which he himself appears to give up when he says that some of the things he wants to treat as private kinds of things are just socially regarded as private. The role of socialization about such matters as sexual intercourse also seems clear in his arguments from the counter-culture for which he has some sympathy. The expectation that the doing of such "typically-done-in-private" kinds of things will not be disclosed to others is also socially conditioned. However, I do not think that it is simply out of recognition that these things are typically done privately in the spatial sense that accounts for our socialized attitude about disclosure. And that is something to which I shall return. But the point I want to make here is that, expectations notwithstanding, the other participant(s) have no duty of nondisclosure. Third, there are other things that do create legitimate (that is, legally enforceable) expectations as to nondisclosure whether or not they are done in private, though they typically are. If there are any private kinds of things at all, these and only these are such things, namely, those things the doing of which does create legal duties of nondisclosure.

While it is not explicit in Wasserstrom's discussion, it does seem implicit that what he wants to argue is that, if there are any private things (that is, things typically done in private and with the expectation of nondisclosure), then these are at least prima facie candidates for privacy. I maintain, however, that these are not even prima facie front-runners unless the expectations they create are legitimate. This is to say nothing more than that the reasons we have for prohibiting intrusions of certain kinds must be independent of judgments about the kinds of things we might have to inquire into. Certainly it is the case that where the other participant(s) have a legal duty of nondisclosure, there also I have a claim-right to privacy. And that is quite different from saying that I ought to have a claim-right to privacy because I am doing a private kind of thing (a thing typically done in private and with the expectation of nondisclosure).

But then we have to settle the far more important question as to when such claim/duty relationships ought to exist, and we are back where we started: Which areas of one's life ought to be free of the scrutiny of others? Typically, of course, it is held to exist in so-called fiduciary relationship where there is a relationship of trust. But bear in mind that this is a contractual trust that is circumscribed by the prohibitions against doing what is illegal (such as contracting for an illegal purpose, counseling the commission of an offense, aiding and abetting, or conspiracy). Thus revelations to my accountant regarding my intent not to declare all of my taxable income are not covered by his duty of nondisclosure. And, of course, if there is deliberate interference with legally private kinds of things —that is, things done in private with the legitimate expectation of nondisclosure—then one has a defense, namely, entrapment or enticement (or at least one does in the United States; these are not defenses in Canada). But the important point here is that many of the things that Wasserstrom wants to call private are certainly not legally private, and I see no reason to base privacy claims of a legal sort on his categories. On the contrary I would think it more sensible to decide which kinds of things we wish to remain or become legally private independently of the question as to whether they happen to be typically done in private and with expectations of nondisclosure.

So now we are back where we started: What kinds of things ought to be protected from scrutiny? And with that I think we are ready to return to some theory. If there are any areas in which one has an inalienable right to freedom, there also one has an inalienable right to privacy. But to my mind, it is impossible to draw any sharp lines demarcating the public from the private so far as the lives of individuals are concerned. It is impossible to say with conviction that there is any part of a person's life that does not, and cannot, have effects on others. There is no area in which the decisions made and the actions taken affect only the interest of the particular individual. Hence, unless some other grounds can be found for drawing this distinction, it cannot be made and hence cannot be used as the basis for defining an area of unrestricted freedom or of unlimited privacy. Thus, to the extent that the underpinnings for an alleged right to privacy rest on defining an area within which persons ought to be able to exercise unlimited freedom because their actions have no consequences for others, it is on shaky ground to say the very least.

But I want now to return to a point I made earlier. Although it does not seem that the fact that there are some activities typically done in private in any way provides guidance as to what ought to be legally private, I think it is of more than passing interest that the kinds of things singled out this way typically are the things that people allege should be legally private. Nor do I think that it is accidental that these are usually activities related to interpersonal relationships, in particular, sexual and familial relationships. Indeed, it is because I have become suspicious of the examples that I am willing to argue that the kind of thing something just typically happens to be is no good reason for providing it the legal protection of privacy. Wasserstrom treated sexual intercourse as the kind of thing that seems to need some legal protections, though he certainly raises some sound objections as to why this attitude should at least be questioned. For him the question is: But if such relationships are not protected, won't we be losing some things we value, in particular, our relative invulnerability, spontaneity, individuality, choice of a life-style, efficiency in handling the various businesses of life, and, more generally "the character of interpersonal relationships"? He says negative freedom, privacy, is "a logically necessary condition for the existence of many of our most meaningful relationships," and I have counted at least five explicit references to the essentially private nature of sexual relationships. Even Prime Minister Trudeau has argued that the state has no business in the bedrooms of the nation. This seems to indicate some rising concern on the part of some that the bedrooms and playrooms of the nation are becoming open territory, for certainly the home, hearth, and harem are historic areas of privacy ensured by the ownership of property. The family lives of the poor have, of course, always been open territory, at least in the sense that nobody felt any obligation to leave them alone or to refrain from making judgments about the terrible moral standards evidenced by their failing to refrain from sexual relations in front of children. But more significantly, rich or poor, the family was regarded as sacrosanct so far as social intervention was concerned. The poor may have been thought to be immoral but until fairly recently nothing much was done to protect the wives and children who were suffering in these familial situations. The male is still regarded as lord of his domain, and the subjects of his domain have virtually no rights to protect themselves against his tyrannical behavior. Indeed, Rousseau insists that it is a wife's duty to put up with her husband's brutish behavior should it turn out that he is not the hoped-for benevolent dictator. To be somewhat brief, male and female relationships both within and without the home and the relationships of husband and wife, husband and children, have typically been held private and none of the law's business.

This attitude seems somewhat surprising. It is now becoming increasingly evident that wife beating, incest, and child abuse are widely practiced. It is also evident to most researchers that very little is done to alleviate the situation. When a group of women in England recently established a center for women to provide them with temporary housing and assistance in the event of divorce, separation, eviction, and so forth, they were amazed at the numbers of women who came to them seeking help.

Before the new coat of paint had dried on the cracked walls of the centre, the first woman and her children arrived. They came, not for immediate advice, but for refuge. They had been beaten by the woman's husband and needed shelter and help. . . . Letters poured in. "My husband's been beating me for twenty (or twenty-five or thirty) years. He'd kill me if he knew I'd written to you—he's a prominent barrister."[4]

And so it goes. There are thousands of battered wives, with no place to go and no one to give them any help, terrified to complain, and getting no relief when they do. Research suggests that incest is on the increase. I doubt that; it is just that people are beginning to talk about it. But it certainly is widespread, and, Freud notwithstanding, it is the fathers who commit the incest, usually running through all the female members of the family in turn. Child abuse of other forms has now become so common that some remedies have been sought, but so far little has been done beyond research. There are reasons why this is so. As was pointed out in a recent study of the problem in metropolitan Toronto, the Children's Aid rarely removes such children from the home, and police interventions rarely lead to anything more than a talk to the abusive parent.

The lack of participation of abusive parents in the criminal justice system is apparently the result of a desire to maintain the notion of family solidarity. This unification cannot be forced. Restrictive and traditional roles do not meet the needs of these children or, indeed, of the parents. The family is not a sacred environment when children are being deliberately harmed. The complicity of our service organizations in child abuse must end.[5]

Enough has been said about rape recently that virtually everyone knows that women are not considered to be entitled to the same legal protections as men so far as their sexual relations are concerned. Indeed, in Canada they are not as well off as beasts. Under the criminal code, bestiality carries a sentence of ten years and requires no corroboration; indecent assault, male, carries ten years and requires no corroboration; indecent assault, female, however, carries five years and requires corroboration.

It seems obvious that the areas in which the law does belong is in the family and in intersexual personal relationships, and its interference certainly ought not to be on the side of according a claim-right to privacy with respect to these relationships, since this will not only permit but condone such behavior. Wasserstrom points out in his arguments from the counterculture that "we have accepted the idea that many things are shameful unless done in private." The irony is that such shameful things go on just because they are left in private. And the same thing is true about sexual relationships outside the home. It is quite clear whose interest has been served by setting the family off as private, and it is equally clear that those interests will only be further entrenched if a claim-right to privacy is accorded in such areas. It is, I think, a supreme irony that the first area in which such a right should be accorded is in that of male homosexuality. The concept behind this judgment is that nothing sexual should be prohibited between consenting adults. Clearly what is meant here is that if two equal adults consent to a certain practice, it should be nobody's business but their own. But since women are not now regarded as the equals of men, to set relationships between them off as private is merely to encourage a fundamental inequality.

The family has historically, both in political and legal theory, been simply assumed as the domain of male dominance. It has never been regarded as a political institution, and the entities who are relegated to it are not members of the political community. As such, women qua reproducers and children have had no political rights. It seems obvious that this state simply reflects a fundamental truth that is only now beginning to surface—that the whole tradition of Western political and legal philosophy already presumes the fundamental inequality of the sexes and the dominance of the male. But the truth has surfaced. Thus, in reply to the set of questions that Wasserstrom raises, my answer is unequivocally, yes; the nature of our interpersonal and familial relationships, at least between the sexes, will change, indeed must change, and if that means that men will no longer be able to appear to be invulnerable supermen in the eyes of the world, no longer able to enjoy the presumption that knowledge as to their sexual and personal inadequacies will not be broadcast to the world, no longer able to choose a life-style that depends on exercising dominance over women, no longer able to claim an individuality that necessitates the total denial of individuality to a woman, no longer able to deny their role in the reproductive function in favor of a more efficient getting on with the business of the world, then so much the worse for them, for these are exactly the kinds of changes that must and will come about. Thus, areas that have been traditionally kept private certainly are not those that should be kept that way; to do so is only to serve further the ideology of male dominance that underlies our most basic thinking about political and legal matters. Insofar as negative freedom in these areas is a defense of sexual privilege, it must be sacrificed in the interest of sexual equality. If privacy in these areas really is a necessary condition of "some of our most meaningful relationships," then it certainly must go too since it is men and not women who have found them to be "meaningful." In the face of the facts, it says precious little that is favorable about the present nature of those relationships.

### III

There are more kinds of privilege in our society than sexual privilege, and even if those things traditionally thought of as private are not those that we wish to see further entrenched as legally private, we still have to consider whether any such things should be legally private. Are there any areas that ought to be beyond the scope of the law's interference? And, if so, is this compatible with a public right to knowledge? I say that an individual claim to privacy is not inconsistent with a public right to knowledge and that it is necessary for the promotion of equality. Thus, the weakest form of my position would be that, even if an individual claim to privacy were incompatible with a public right to knowledge, the limitation of the public right to knowledge is justified since it is necessary to the promotion of equality. As I argued earlier, those with privacy are in a privileged position with respect to gaining those social goods we believe to be desirable. Some people already have a greater ability to further their economic and social interest as a consequence of their privacy, and thus an equal right to privacy is a necessary condition of limiting the privacy of some in order to promote the privacy, and hence the economic and social interest, of others. Each person has a moral interest in maintaining his or her freedom, that is, in having at least some areas private and free of restraint; each individual has a right to restraints on others without which there is no positive freedom or access to information that is necessary to an equal opportunity to pursue economic and social interests.

Thus, all persons have an interest, a moral interest, in privacy insofar as that is seen as a negative quality, being left free of restraint, and some have an economic and social interest in privacy insofar as it would limit the positive freedom some others already have to pursue their economic and social good on the basis of privileged information. Needless to say, those others have an economic interest in preventing the remainder from limiting their privacy and in preventing the extension of privacy to that remainder. Limitations of privacy would lead to the legal requirement for disclosure of what would otherwise be privileged information, and extension of the right to privacy to others would limit the information that could be gathered about them and put to the use of those who presently control it. Both things would clearly destroy the privileged position that the elite now enjoys.

In some areas, there should be greater disclosure in order to promote equal access to the information necessary to pursue one's social good. Just as the interest of women and children can be served only by opening up areas that have hitherto been covered by the privilege-right of privacy, so also can the interest of those who have been denied equal access to information be served only by opening up those areas that have allowed an elite to concentrate economic and political power in its own hands. What kinds of information do people need to have in order to make intelligent choices about their public officials and policies and about their own economic interest? The most obvious things they need to know are those surrounding the financial and economic interests of private legal persons; by this I mean corporations as well as natural persons. What someone's financial interests are should be a matter of public knowledge. Why not establish a public records office whose function would be to solicit and keep accurate records as to the financial interests of all legal persons? Such records would, of course, be subject to the perusal and correction of the individual whose record it is but would be open to everyone. This would need to include information as to membership on boards of corporations, interlocking directorates, outlines of conglomerate corporate structures, and all the features necessary to a full delineation of the economic structure and resources of our society.

A second area in which there should be greater disclosure of information is that surrounding the operation of professional societies. Clearly not all such information should be public. Professional organizations such as medical, bar, and accountants' associations, can and should have the power to discipline their own members and to enforce agreed-upon standards of professional conduct. However, when members have been found to fall short of the standards of the reasonably competent practitioner of the discipline, this, too, should be a matter of public knowledge. The public has a right to be protected from incompetent practitioners who presently operate behind the veil of professionalism.

A third area that ought to be open to the public is that surrounding the structure and operation of governmental agencies, departments, and institutions supported by public funds, such as hospitals, prisons, and universities. Obviously, again, not all such information should have to be publicly disclosed. Although I think that much gets hidden behind the alleged need for national defense or security, I am certainly prepared to acknowledge that there may well be some areas in which this is a genuine concern. However, private information ought to be the exception rather than the rule. I am making no claims as to having delineated all the areas about which there should be full or partial disclosure in the interest of the public good, but these at least are some of the major ones. The basic point is that we must create a more open society if all the members of it are to have equal access to information and hence to economic and political power. The basic principle that should guide our choices ought to be that nothing is in principle private, since there are no areas of one's private or public life that are in principle incapable of affecting the interests of others.

But what then is to be left to the discretion of individuals? Obviously, if the assumption is that nothing is by nature private, we cannot identify particular areas in which one should be protected by a legal claim to privacy. We need a somewhat new approach to this question. We need to ask ourselves new questions. The first one is: What is it that we wish to protect ourselves from? Who or what is the enemy? We are all too well aware of the rapid establishment of what Wasserstrom has referred to as a data-bank society, in which virtually all of the things we do could be kept track of, without our knowledge, not subject to our perusal, and disseminated without our consent. Each of us wants to retain control over personal information that could be used to our disadvantage. The areas in which this is now either a reality or a distinct possibility are too numerous to list. One of the best accounts of the many abuses in the collection and dissemination of information regarding private individuals is that given in the *Report of the Committee on Privacy*.[6] Much greater regulation, backed up by stiff sanctions, is needed. The basic principle ought to be that all information disclosed in connection with facilitating any of our daily business should be held to be a trust relationship and should create a duty of nondisclosure. So that individuals are allowed the right to do that which is not injurious to the rights of others, the collection of information should be prohibited about individuals by other legal individuals where the individual does not have the right of access to that information, lacks opportunity to rebut data that might be seriously prejudicial, and has no opportunity to exercise control over its dissemination.

In conclusion, the values of freedom and equality of opportunity with respect to participation in the political process require as wide a dissemination to the public of information as is possible. Thus, the alleged right of an individual to privacy ought not to be used to keep required information out of the public domain. On the other hand, because some private individuals are more powerful than others and there is a preexisting state of inequality between individual members of society, some controls have to be imposed to prevent some people from collecting information about others where such information has a bearing on the interests of the individual in question and over which he has no control. Thus, there is a need for claim-rights to privacy established by means of stringent regulations on all those persons, agencies, and institutions who collect such information and by the establishment of a new tort. It would be somewhat pointless to protect the public from the censorship of the elite while leaving individuals powerless to resist the unrestrained demands of others who hold power over their lives. It is scant remedy to be saved from the whale only to be eaten by the piranha fish.

## Notes

1. Some of this material was originally presented as part of a symposium on the philosophy of law, devoted to the topic, "The Individual Right to Privacy vs. A Public Right to Knowledge," delivered at the Annual Meeting of the Canadian Philosophical Association, University of Toronto, June 1, 1974.
2. Since I think that nothing but confusion can result from failing to distinguish what kind of rights we are alleging either to exist or to be desirable, I am utilizing the distinctions made by W. N. Hohfeld, *Fundamental Legal Conceptions* (New Haven: Yale University Press, 1946), in order to try to clarify these issues.
3. For example, see the untitled paper delivered by D. Weisstub to the Annual Meeting of the Canadian Philosophical Society.
4. Gay Search, "London: Battered Wives," *Ms.* (June 1974).
5. Bonnie Rose, "An Exploratory Investigation into the Nature of Child Abuse" (Master's thesis, University of Toronto, 1974), p. 49.
6. *Report of the Committee on Privacy,* under the Chairmanship of the Rt. Hon. Kenneth Younger (London: Her Majesty's Stationery Office, 1972).

# 15

# Children and privacy

**HOWARD COHEN**

The lack of privacy is a rather painful and almost pervasive fact of life for most children. A child's personal possessions are not safe from inspection by parents at home, teachers and other officials at school, or the police on the streets. Pockets, drawers, desks, rooms, lockers, automobile trunks, and other personal places are not sacrosanct in the child's world; they are open and available to sufficiently curious adults. Such invasions of privacy are well established in custom and often sanctioned in law as well. Agents of the state are often empowered to maintain files of personal, educational, medical, and legal information on children and to distribute that information as they see fit. Although this reality touches some children more than others, no children are very secure from such invasions. Furthermore, these intrusions into children's lives are not regarded as violations of rights. Similar treatment of adults would quite properly raise a storm of protest that civil and human rights were being violated. But children are not thought of as having any right to privacy at all. For them, privacy is, at best, a privilege enjoyed at the pleasure of adults. Should the adult wish to revoke it, the child has no recourse.

Whatever the reasons that children are treated this way in our society, our conception of rights, and the right to privacy in particular, serves to underscore the practice and provide some justification for it. In the liberal tradition of political philosophy, which has come down fairly well intact since the seventeenth century and remains at the theoretical center of our present-day legal system, rights are defined in terms of what is now called negative freedom. H. L. A. Hart has drawn the connection in this way:

And it is I think a very important feature of a moral right that the possessor of it is conceived as having a moral justification for limiting the freedom of

another and that he has this justification not because the action he is entitled to require of another has some moral quality but simply because in the
circumstances a certain distribution of human freedom will be maintained
if he by his choice is allowed to determine how that other shall act.[1]

These moral rights, then, delimit the freedom of others and in the
process establish a system of spheres of mutual noninterference.
By determining that others may not act in a particular way, I reserve
the prerogative of doing or having something for myself. Others, of
course, may also determine how I shall act so they can exercise a
similar prerogative. Our interlocking system of negative freedoms
defines the rights each of us has in society.

This conception of a system of rights requires a good deal from
those who have them. One must be able to exercise freedom. And
this requires a rather well-developed will and sufficient intellect to
understand one's place in the distribution of human freedoms.
Most writers in this tradition have assumed that children are not
sufficiently developed in these respects to warrant according rights
to them. John Locke argues this point extensively in "Of Paternal
Power" in the *Second Treatise of Civil Government*. In "On
Liberty," John Stuart Mill does not think that the point really
merits much argument. After insisting on the absolute right of the
individual to independence in areas that concern only himself, Mill
remarks: "It is, perhaps, hardly necessary to say that this doctrine
is meant to apply only to human beings in the maturity of their fac-
ulties. We are not speaking of children, of young persons below the
age which the law may fix as that of manhood or womanhood."[2]
Mill's view remains the conventional wisdom both in custom and in
law. Only recently have child advocates such as Richard Farson
and John Holt suggested that children and adults not be treated differently with regard to the rights they enjoy.[3]

If rights in general are to be analyzed in terms of negative freedom, the right to privacy is in some ways the clearest case. Lorenne
M. G. Clark has made this point explicitly in "Privacy, Property,
Freedom, and the Family." "Discussions as to whether there ought
to be a legally entrenched right to privacy seem to me to be virtually
identical to the disputes in philosophy as to whether there should
be an area of one's life in which one has an unlimited right to freedom." And a little later on: "Negative freedom is the freedom to do

what I want, to be unrestricted in the pursuit of my interests as I see them. One could go so far as to say that the right to being let alone, or private, is virtually identical with the right to unimpeded activity, or negative freedom." Once privacy is identified with negative freedom, the whole weight of the liberal political tradition stands against a right of privacy for children.

In the face of this, I shall argue that children ought to have some rights over their privacy and that they should enjoy these rights to the same extent that adults do. I do not wish to make this claim for all of the things that have been called the right to privacy, but I insist on some fairly significant rights (for example, the right to keep information about oneself confidential). Because the right to privacy has been so closely associated with the notion of negative freedom, it will be necessary to make the argument for a child's right to privacy at a more general level. There is nothing particularly unique about privacy that children should have a right to it as an exception to the general practice. Indeed, as we have seen, privacy is, if anything, the paradigm right. My aim, therefore, is to argue more comprehensively for equal rights for children. In the course of the argument I shall call into question the relevance of the differences between children and adults for the granting of rights. This, in turn, requires raising questions about the adequacy of the analysis of rights in terms of negative freedom.

Advocating children's rights does not automatically set one against the whole liberal political tradition. In fact, those interested in the rights of children have divided into two camps. Some argue that children need special protection in a world dominated by adults who care little for their interests. Adherents of this older branch of the children's rights movement have stood at the forefront of the drives for child labor laws, compulsory education, restrictions on corporal punishment, juvenile court reform, and the like. More recently, though, a second notion of children's rights has developed, which stands in opposition to special protection. Adherents of the equal treatment position wish to extend to children social respect and most of the legal rights presently enjoyed by adults. Practically this means, among other things, that children may work without special restriction, avoid school if they choose, manage their own money, own property, and vote. Those in the equal treatment camp tend to see special protection as a kind of paternalism, which they find constraining and inhibiting. Richard Farson puts the difference this way:

Liberating children, giving them equality, and guaranteeing their civil rights, may seem to violate the fairly recent realizations that children are not simply miniature adults, and that childhood is a special time of life, with special qualities and problems. In fact, never before in history have parents and teachers had so much "understanding" of children, or at least of their physical and social development. But the "understanding" has led not to improved conditions for children, but simply to more control of them and consequently more burdensome responsibilities of supervision for parents.[4]

Farson sees equal treatment for children as a way out from under this burden. The core of his position is that children should have the right to self-determination. In other words, "Children should have the right to decide the matters which affect them most directly."[5] As examples, Farson offers choosing one's environment, securing information, educating oneself, and exercising economic and political power. John Holt argues in the same vein and produces a list of rights for children that is in many ways similar to Farson's. He states that children should have "the right to do, in general, what any adult may legally do" and "the right to privacy" (which he does not discuss in detail).[6]

The Farson-Holt position does not accord well with our sensibilities about proper behavior for children. Most adults find it difficult to comprehend what it might mean for a three- or five- or even a ten-year-old child to have a right to political power, economic self-determination, or privacy. Yet in spite of this Farson and Holt ought not to be dismissed as part of the lunatic fringe. There is a point to equal rights for children.

The main difficulty with their position is that the obvious argument for extending equal rights to some deprived group is inappropriate. Typically a principle of fairness—that similar cases be treated similarly—is invoked. Where differences between those having the rights and those deprived are not relevantly difference making, there is no justification for discrimination. This may be the case for some rights that should be extended to children, but it will not do for rights based on self-determination.

When it comes to self-determination, privacy, political power, and the like, adults and children do appear to differ in relevant ways. Adults have capacities for understanding and action that are not yet developed—or not adequately developed— in children. The specific capacities in question may differ from right to right, of course, but the objection to equal treatment has been put quite generally. It is rationality that is undeveloped—or underdeveloped—in children, and the fact that a child is not rational is taken as a reason to withhold from her or him rights that are accorded to adults. This argument has been around for a long time, receiving its fullest and most considered articulation in John Locke's *Second Treatise of Civil Government*. Since it is the most common—and most serious objection to equal treatment for children—it deserves a closer look.

Locke argues that children are born *to* the state of equality, though not in it.[7] The reason is that as infants they are "weak and helpless, without knowledge or understanding."[8] As Locke makes clear shortly, this means that they are without the use of reason and thus not under the law of reason. Hence, he argues, children are not free, for the use of reason is a necessary condition for freedom. He establishes the connection this way: "For law, in its true notion, is not so much the limitation as the direction of a free and intelligent agent to his proper interests, and prescribes no further than is for the general good."[9] That is, without a developed reason, one cannot discern proper areas of action and make choices within their compass. The result is that a parent or guardian is obligated to act for the child until such a time as the child has sufficient reason to exercise her or his then acquired rights:

But while he is in an estate wherein he has not understanding of his own to direct his will, he is not to have any will of his own to follow; he that understands for him must will for him too; he must prescribe to his will and regulate his actions; but when he comes to the estate that made his father a freeman, the son is a freeman too.[10]

Locke puts the age of reason at "twenty-one, and in some cases sooner."[11]

Locke's argument goes to the heart of the Farson-Holt position since they make self-determination the crux of equal treatment. If

self-determination requires rationality and children are not rational, it is hard to see what can be said for children's rights. To meet
this argument it will be necessary to develop it a bit, but before
doing so we must set aside two tempting but ultimately unsatisfactory objections. In the first place, one might argue that Locke
has set the age of reason arbitrarily high. There is little doubt these
days that the typical eighteen year old has sufficient understanding
to direct her will if the typical twenty-one year old does. The cam-
paign to lower the age of majority made judicious use of this fact.
Surely there is no way to date the age of reason precisely. No proposed set of characteristics of rationality will separate most twenty
year olds from most twenty-one year olds. For that matter, even if
we ignore the fact that members of a group may develop at different
rates, it is highly implausible that such a set of characteristics
could even pick out the moment of rationality in a single individual.
Rationality is not the sort of thing that one acquires in a moment.
But in spite of the fact that dating the attainment of rationality is
highly arbitrary, few would be inclined to take this to its bitter end.
The fact that reason is developed over time makes date setting an
arbitrary pastime, but it also precludes the assumption that one
has it at birth. The two year old does not have sufficient understanding to direct her will—at least not with respect to the areas of
activity Farson and Holt specify. Yet Farson and Holt are not interested in lowering the age of self-determination, privacy, political
power, and so on; they want to abolish line drawing for equal
rights. And since they do not wish to restrict these rights to the
"rational" child, this rejoinder would not be open to them. For their
purposes, Locke's arbitrariness is not sufficient to discount the
argument.

The second standard objection to this argument is presented as a
reductio ad absurdum. If a developed reason is a necessary condition for many or most rights, then it is not only children who ought
to be controlled. Most adults sometimes, and many adults usually,
do not have sufficient understanding to perceive and act on their
"proper interests." It would seem that Locke is committed to denying them rights too. Although this consequence might violate our
sense of democracy, it is not entirely devastating. On the one hand,
one might still quibble about how much understanding is enough.

Locke never said that we must be entirely clear about the bounds of our freedom. And on the other hand, in some cases (lunatics and idiots) Locke is willing to accept the implications of his position and deny rights to adults.[12] While this may be objectionable, it is not obviously absurd even today, and it was certainly not absurd in the seventeenth century. The outcome may, however, drive the Lockean to defend equal rights for competent people of whatever age. Nevertheless Farson and Holt want all children to have equal rights—competent or not—so this line of attack will not serve them well either. To make their case, one must show that rationality is not a difference-making difference. This requires confrontation, not deflection.

Locke's argument makes the connection between rights and rationality through the concept of freedom. By freedom he means "a liberty to dispose and order as he lists his person, actions, possessions, and his whole property, *within the allowance of those laws under which he is,* and therein not be subject to the arbitrary will of another."[13] Today this notion is termed negative freedom; it circumscribes areas of action for the individual where others may not interfere.

As we have noted, in the classical liberal tradition, the boundaries of negative freedom mark off the area of individual rights, that is, within the area of negative freedom, the individual may act as she or he sees fit without prohibition or interference from others. Under such circumstances it is fairly easy to see why Locke would deny rights to the nonrational. Reason is required both to discern boundaries and to guide choice within them. The absence of rationality, therefore, renders rights pointless or harmful. They are pointless if the bearer of the right lacks capacities required to exercise it. To take an example from Farson, children should have the right to choose from among alternative home environments. But a one year old barely has a notion of what a home environment is, much less a concept of alternatives. In order for the Lockean to acknowledge a right here, the child would have to be able to assess the relative merits of the alternatives, perceive her own proper interests, and act on the basis of that understanding. Anything short of this is not a freely willed choice—and the one-year-old child falls considerably short owing to the lack of a developed reason. Since such a person could not conceivably exercise Farson's right, conferring it would be frivolous. A slightly older child may be sufficiently endowed with understanding and skills to know how to leave home, but even here the Lockean would argue against the child's right to an alternative home environment. The ability to leave home is not indicative of the ability to understand alternatives and select the one that is in the child's proper interests. Harm might be done if adults could not interfere with rash decisions made on the basis of undeveloped capacities. Moreover, harm might be done to others if the child does not understand the limits of the right and acts so as to encroach on another's freedom. The child may not realize that she cannot live just anywhere and move in on others for whom her presence would be a hardship.

The foundation of this argument is a conception of rights that embodies a principle of noninterference:

I.   $A$ has a right to $X$ implies Everyone has an obligation not to interfere with $A$'s obtaining or exercising $X$.

With this notion of rights and considerations of pointlessness and harmfulness, it is possible to build a case against extending many of Farson's proposed rights to children. Take, for example, the right to information. Farson says, "A child must have the right to all information ordinarily available to adults—including, and perhaps especially, information that makes adults uncomfortable."[14] Presumably this means children should have access to psychological tests, academic records (including teachers' evaluations), medical records, and the like. But what is the point of conferring this right on the child who cannot read or understand the significance of the information? Why should anyone be obligated to stand aside as the child leafs through incomprehensible records? To the Lockean, Farson's insistence on equal rights here is a meaningless gesture. But what is worse, as the child develops, the gesture becomes potentially dangerous. Perhaps a child might partially understand such information but misconstrue it sufficiently to do herself psychological damage. No possible good would be served, the argument goes, by extending such a right to children. A similar case can be made against many of Farson's proposed rights and

Holt's as well. Self-determination, self-education, privacy, political and economic power: in each case, barely rational children do not have the capacities to act in these areas, and children of limited rationality cannot do so safely. In neither situation is the insistence on noninterference justified, so in neither situation should the child be accorded the right.

Although this argument expresses a proper concern for children's welfare, it seems to depend too heavily upon a very limited conception of rights. The plausibility of the claims that the granting of such rights would be harmful or pointless requires the assumption that adults must not interefere with the child's activity. But why must all rights be thought of as marking the boundaries of negative freedom? In fact, many rights cannot be assimilated to this model. I submit that there is another notion of rights that can be shown to apply to many of the Farson-Holt cases and that makes the demand for equal treatment possible.

Many rights, of course, imply the principle of noninterference. But that principle is not sufficient to explain a large number of rights generally conceded and legally protected. Some rights obligate particular people to aid the claimant in specifiable ways. That is, they imply a principle of performance:

II. *A* has a right to *X* implies Someone has an obligation to help *A* obtain or exercise *X*.

Naturally the individual(s) obligated and the extent of the obligation must be specified for each right. For example, if *A* has a right to vote, then *A*'s employer has an obligation to give *A* time off from work to vote. This obligation is not merely the employer's own special way of not interfering with *A*'s right. So long as *A* could vote before or after working hours, the employer could rightly claim that keeping *A* at the job did not actually interfere with the opportunity to exercise the right. This is so, and it shows that the employer's obligation runs beyond noninterference; that principle cannot satisfactorily explain the right, which implies that some people must make it convenient for *A* to vote. So while noninterference and performance may provide some sort of continuum of obligations, there are many cases in which the obligations attending the right go well beyond stepping aside.

In seventeenth-century England one might have been hard pressed to find rights that implied a principle of performance. In theory and in law noninterference was about as much as anyone was required to do in the face of the rights of others. Consequently Locke may be excused for failing to think of children's rights in any other terms. There is less excuse these days, however, as a growing body of rights—moral and legal—are obligating people to aid claimants in securing their rights.

One area in which the transition from rights based on the first principle to rights based on the second is particularly clear is that of trial rights. In the eighteenth century, the right to counsel in criminal trials was taken to mean that the state could not prevent a defendant from having a lawyer (should the defendant be willing and able to secure one). Eventually this right was reinterpreted to the point where today states are obligated to provide counsel for indigent defendants in any case that carries a possible prison term.[15] What was once clearly a right of noninterference is presently one of performance. A similar transition could be traced in the area of consumer's rights. The principle of caveat emptor explicitly absolved merchant and manufacturer of any obligations of performance. Today consumers do not enjoy their rights so unmercifully. Contracts may even be voided if the merchant fails to provide certain information. The effect of this is to specify performance obligations for consumer's rights. Thus, where having a right in the seventeenth century entitled one to be let alone, it may, in the twentieth century, entitle one to a certain amount of aid in securing it.[16] With this possibility in mind we can reexamine the case for equal rights for children.

In the case of performance rights, it is not so clear that it would be harmful or pointless to grant them to persons not fully rational. That would seem to depend upon who was obligated to help the child and to what extent. But before this can be spelled out, it is necessary to address the·question of whether there are any reasons to treat the Farson-Holt proposals as performance rights. We may not suppose that these ought to be children's rights simply because they could be. But, in fact, there is an excellent reason to regard many of them as implying a principle of performance and extending them to children.

Those who argue against the equal treatment of children on the grounds of their lack of rationality are surely committed to a developmental view of capacities—reason included. That view is hardly controversial. Neither, for that matter, is the further assumption that this development is due to, or at least advanced by, experience. Locke certainly accepted these claims, and it seems that anyone subscribing to his arguments for parental power is also implicitly committed to them. Yet if this is so, then it seems that many of the rights adults have as noninterference rights, children should have as performance rights. For how but by the exercise of their capacities are children supposed to develop them sufficiently to enter the state of equality? In short, children ought to learn to exercise those rights in becoming adults that they will later exercise as adults—so long as doing this improves rather than retards the capacities in question. That it will so improve them is doubtful if rights imply the principle of noninterference but it is fairly likely if they imply the principle of performance. In the latter case we are no longer faced with the specter of pointless or harmful activity which we are helpless to rectify.

Consider the right to information again. "*A* has the right to information" implies someone has an obligation to help *A* obtain information. To secure the child's rights and help extend her reason, the obligated adult will have to fill the role of educator rather than servant. The obligation cannot be simply to retrieve a file and read the words. The information must be explained to the child in such a way that she can assimilate some of it and begin to assess its value. This will not happen all at once and, no doubt, satisfying the obligation in a safe and meaningful way will be difficult. But we have no business supposing that the mastery of capacities will be easy work. If anything this is yet another reason to grant access to information as a child's right. This way, at least, some adults are obligated to make the effort.

In pressing for equal rights for children, Farson and Holt face the difficulty of developing the capacity to reason and act more squarely than the Lockean. Locke is confident that the child "will come to the estate that made his father a freeman," but he is utterly opaque when it comes to saying how this will happen. Farson realizes that it will happen only through experience that adults may guide but cannot have for children: "It is important that children be given the opportunity to take risks in order to develop, to push their limits, to discover their potential."[17] Through the principle of performance, these risks can be controlled to the point where they will not justify withholding the self-determination rights from children.

There is a danger in arguments such as this one, that one form of paternalism will be substituted for another. Instead of adults acting to protect nonrational children, we will have adults acting to mold the children's capacities in their own image—and this in the name of the development of rationality. The danger can hardly be avoided. In the first place rationality is a somewhat illusive notion; there is bound to be disagreement about how it is exemplified. Second, each right will require its own specifications, both as to who is obligated and in what ways. There is no general way to lay down these obligations for all rights in advance. Often the obligations will depend upon what in a society constitutes an obstacle to the child's development.

Yet in spite of the difficulties, there is at least one feature of rights that affords some protection here. Rights define areas in which claims must be honored, but their exercise is at the discretion of the claimant. A child may have a right yet express no desire to exercise it. For this reason there is no need to place a lower limit on the age at which a child has equal rights. A one year old may have the right to alternative home environments without ever demanding a change. This is perfectly acceptable so long as the child has the right when she is first ready to claim it. It does not really matter when that is, so long as it is marked as an attempt to exercise certain capacities and be treated accordingly. In general, the principle of performance does not impose the obligation to initiate action on the child's behalf. It imposes the obligation to aid the child in fulfilling expressed desires of the requisite sort. To  uard against paternalism one must resist the temptation to postulate "real" or "hidden" (as opposed to expressed) desires in children to exercise capacities they show no overt interest in. This is not a complete safeguard, but it avoids some of the worst abuses. The reference point for adult intervention must always be to aid the child to develop the capability of self-determination rather than to take action for the child or in her name.

So much for rights in general. What of the right to privacy? Can privacy be the sort of thing that others can help one to exercise or attain? This only seems odd if one is thinking of privacy in terms of aloneness, where the very presence of others would seem to violate the right. While this is one sort of privacy that people may have a right to, it is surely not the only—or even the most significant—right that goes by that name. In cases where the right to privacy is the right to confidentiality (information disclosed to another may not be disclosed to a third party without authorization), the analysis of the right in terms of performance makes more sense.

I want now to suggest how the law might be improved by treating privacy as a performance right and extending it to children. In 1973 Massachusetts passed a law providing protective services for abused, injured, or neglected children. One of the main thrusts of the law was to establish a regular reporting procedure for suspected cases of child abuse. Realizing that the state would, in consequence, be collecting sensitive personal information, the legislators made some effort to protect the child's privacy:

*Section 51E* The department shall maintain a file of the written reports prepared pursuant to this section and sections fifty-one A to fifty-one D, inclusive. Such written reports shall be confidential. The child's parent, guardian, or consul, the reporting person or agency, the appropriate review board, or a social worker assigned to the case, may, upon request, and upon the approval of the commissioner, receive a copy of the written report of the initial investigation. No such report shall be made available to any persons other than those enumerated in this section without the written consent of the child's parent or guardian, the written approval of the commissioner, or an order of a court of competent jurisdiction.[18]

By placing the right to protect the confidentiality of the report with the parent, the guardian, or the state rather than with the child, the legislators were following accepted legal practice. The rationale for doing so is by now quite familiar. When someone has the right to decide who may have access to these reports, then everyone else is obligated not to interfere with that decision. If the child is sufficiently undeveloped in will or intellect, it would be pointless to confer this right to her or him. Having the right would not give the child control over the information. For the somewhat more developed child, the right to decide who may have this information could be dangerous, for the information is, by its very nature, sensitive, and the child is likely to use it unwisely. The right to privacy, therefore, must be exercised by the parent in the name of the child. Although this story is familiar, it is not very satisfactory.

The main problem with laws that substitute parental protection for children's rights is that they fail to take into account the possibility that the interests of the parent and the child may conflict. In cases of child abuse, this is more than a remote possibility. Suppose that a twelve-year-old girl has been sexually abused by her father. A neighbor suspects this and makes a report to the police, who in turn refer the matter to a social worker. The social worker makes an investigation and files a report, but the report does not contain sufficient evidence to warrant a criminal complaint. Suppose further that the child's mother wishes to divorce her husband. She would like to use the report of child abuse to strengthen her case and perhaps reach a more lucrative settlement.

It is in the father's interest to maintain the confidentiality of the report and in the mother's interest to make it a matter of record in a court proceeding. Under the circumstances, it is hard to imagine that either one could protect the child. What would be in the child's interest in a case like this? We would have to know whether the child wished to maintain some kind of relationship with her father and whether allowing her mother to use the report would preclude that possibility. We would also need to know whether the child would find the use of such information in a divorce proceeding sufficiently humiliating to make a relationship with her mother impossible. But it is not just that we would need to know this; the child needs to know it as well. And we may not presume that she does, or could, know it without having gone through some decision-making process. In other words, the decision about whether to release the information may require that the child has thought the matter through and made a choice.

If it is plausible to say, in some cases at least, that it would be better if the child could make the decision about the confidentiality of the information than to leave the child under parental protection in this regard, then our problem is how to put the child in the best position to make the decision. Here we may draw on the principle of performance: to say that the child has a right to privacy is to say that someone has an obligation to help the child exercise it. That person need not be the parent or any one lifelong designate for that matter. It ought to be someone who does not have a conflict of interest with the child and who is committed to using the occasion of the exercise of a right to develop the child's capacities for self-determination.

If we begin to think of rights less exclusively in terms of negative freedom and more often in terms of the principle of performance, we will find that it is not necessary to draw so many arbitrary and demeaning distinctions between adults and children. We will be able to give the notion of human development its due in the social and legal spheres and give up the fiction that people inexplicably come of age at some designated moment in their lives. Clearly, I am not arguing that children should be treated as if they were adults. My point is that we do not need to deny these differences in a workable conception of rights. Many rights that adults enjoy can be enjoyed by children as well—and it is about time that some of them were.

## Notes

1. H. L. A. Hart, "Are There Any Natural Rights?" in *Human Rights,* ed. A. I. Melden (Belmont, Calif.: Wadsworth, 1970), p. 64.
2. John Stuart Mill, *On Liberty* (Indianapolis: Bobbs-Merrill, 1956), p. 13.
3. There is a growing literature on children's rights, but as a social movement, it has only recently gained attention, is not particularly powerful, and is still without a sufficiently developed theoretical base. Some of the most notable writings in this area are Richard Farson, *Birthrights* (New York: Macmillan, 1974) and John Holt, *Escape from Childhood* (New York: Ballantine Books, 1974). Farson's child's bill of rights is:

    1. The Right to Self-Determination
    2. The Right to Alternative Home Environments
    3. The Right to Responsive Design

4. The Right to Information
5. The Right to Educate Oneself
6. The Right to Freedom from Physical Punishment
7. The Right to Sexual Freedom
8. The Right to Economic Power
9. The Right to Political Power
10. The Right to Justice

4. Farson, *Birthrights,* p. 67.
5. Ibid., pp. 68-69.
6. Holt, *Escape,* p. 2.
7. John Locke, *The Second Treatise of Civil Government* (Indianapolis: Bobbs-Merrill, 1952), p. 31.
8. Ibid., p. 32.
9. Ibid.
10. Ibid., p. 33.
11. Ibid., p. 34.
12. Ibid.
13. Ibid., p. 33. (Emphasis added.)
14. Farson, *Birthrights,* pp. 68-69.
15. The right is articulated in *Gideon* v. *Wainright.* The transition is admirably documented in A. Lewis, *Gideon's Trumpet* (New York: Random House, 1964).
16. Obviously many rights imply only a principle of noninterference.
17. Farson, *Birthrights,* p. 71.
18. Acts and Resolves of the Commonwealth of Massachusetts, Acts, 1973, Chapter 1076, Section 51E.

# Index

Elites, 146, 171-73, 185, 187

Entrapment, 179

**Equality:** in access to information, 171-72, 183; before the law, 87; for children, 191-202; concept of, 57, 82-83; of opportunity,'48, 53, 59, 89, 124-25, 145, 171-73, 184; as a social ideal, 50, 60, 71-72, 81, 91; and special status for Indians, 86-87; in the trial process, 124-25, 133-37. *See also* Rights

Equal Protection Clause (Fourteenth Amendment to the U. S. Constitution), 52, 57, 60, 72, 90

Evidence, problems of adducing, 109-11, 117, 124-25, 131-36. *See also* Legal competence

Farson, Richard, 189 passim

Foot, Philippa, 30-33

Forsey, Eugene, 84

Frank, Jerome, 106, 109-13, 115, 117, 130-31

Frankel, Marvin, 107, 109-10, 112-13, 117

Fredegund, Queen, 96

Freedman, Monroe, 112, 114, 117

Freedom: of conscience, 175; of information, 144-45; negative, 143-44, 146, 168-70, 173, 180, 184, 188-90, 194, 196, 202; positive, 184

Friedrich, Carl Joachim, 137

Fuller, Lon L., 105, 116

Gordon, Murray, 109

Gregory of Tours, 96

Hall, Emmett, 86, 88

Hart, H. L. A., 39, 42, 188

*Hickman* v. *Taylor*, 98

Hohfeld, W. N., 187

Holt, John, 189 passim

Homosexuality, 68, 155, 182

Illegal search, 155, 188

Illocutionary and perlocutionary acts, 36, 43

Incest, 144, 163, 180, 201

Individual personhood, 154, 175-76

Information as property, 171

Juvenile court, 117, 137, 190

Kant, I., 71

Kelsen, Hans, 108

Laskin, Bora, 87-88

*Lavell* case, 87

Lawyers and philosophers, 127-30

Legal aid, 50, 137

Legal competence, 110, 115-16, 124, 134-35, 185

Liberalism, 53, 168, 171, 188-90

Llewellyn, Karl N., 99, 102

Locke, John, 189, 192-98

Lowell, A. L., 62

Lucas, John, 14

Lukes, S., 29

Male chauvinism, 144, 182-83

Mayer, Martin, 112, 114

Meritocratic (meritarian) criteria, 49, 56, 59-60, 70, 72, 82

Mill, John Stuart, 68, 78-80, 189

Minnesota Supreme Court, 115

Moses Maimonides, 115

Northrop, F. C. S., 129

*Parteibetreib*, 105

Paternalism, 78, 190-91, 199, 201

Plato: *Politeia*, 41; *Republic*, 80, 111

Plea bargaining, 102

Policies, economic and noneconomic, 47-49, 54-72, 74, 78-79, 88, 125

Power: as ability to order, 32-33; brute or sheer, 3-4, 33, 37-39; conferment of, 4, 15, 20; as influence, 10-11, 29, 37; information as, 171-72; normative, 4-5, 10, 14, 18-22, 31, 32-33, 35; over oneself and others, 20-22; -utterances, 17-20

Preferences: 66-72, 75-83; altruistic, 67, 70, 81; associational, 69-71, 73; external, 49, 66-68, 71, 75, 81-83; including political, 67-68; instrumental, 71; moralistic, 67-69; personal, 66-68, 70, 80

Preferential treatment, 47-48, 50-51, 53, 57, 59, 72, 74-79, 84, 87-88, 90

Pretrial discovery, 111, 124, 132, 135-36

Principle of noninterference, a, 195-202

Principle of performance, a, 196-202

Privacy: absolutist conception, 144, 179; of arrest records, 142, 159-60; bodily, 150-51, 173-74, 188; children's, 188-202; as a claim-right, 145-46, 161, 169-70, 178, 199; conceived spatially, 171, 177-78; as a defeasible concept, 169; and the effect of being observed, 156-57, 161-63, 177, 180; in family relations, 144, 146, 179-82; and financial interests, 184-85; legal right of, 145-46, 167, 169-70, 173-79, 183-87, 200-02; mental, 149-50, 153-55, 163-64, 173-75; and a new tort, 187; of personal data, 141-42, 145, 157-61, 186, 190, 200; and the poor, 180; and the private kind of thing, 145, 152, 155-56, 159-62, 173, 183-87; and the public's right to know, 170-72,

183-87, 195; in sexual relations, 143, 146, 149, 151-52, 156, 164-65, 177, 179, 180-83; and things done in private, 151-52, 155, 176-79; value of, 162-65, 167, 171-73, 202

Psychotherapy, 150

Punishment, 39, 96, 190

Quintilian, 112

Quotas, 48, 53, 90

Rape, 181-82

Rationality, the concept of, 6-7, 28, 31. See also Authority, paradoxes of

Rawls, John, 128, 130

Raz, Joseph, 128-29

**Reasons:** absolute and prima facie, 15, 17, 23, 36; for action, 17-18, 32-34, 36, 39; advice, orders, and requests as, 15-17, 22-27, 30-31, 35-37, 43; balance of, 5-7, 16, 23-28, 31, 34-35, see Rights, Policies; complete, 30-31; conflicting, 22-24, see Rights, and utility; exclusionary, 5, 18-20, 22-23, 27-28, 31, 34-36, 43; first-order, 23, 27, 34-36, 41; kind and weight in, 16, 23-25, 36; protected, 5, 19-24, 31-32; second-order, see Reasons, exclusionary; weighty, 16, 23-24, 36

Reverse discrimination. See Preferential treatment

**Rights:** absolutely equal, 49, 57; abstract legal, 57; against self-incrimination, 154; Canadian Bill of, 86-88; child's bill of, 203; to command, see Authority; counsel's, 134; to equal treatment and consideration, 49, 54, 57-58, 74-76, 80, 82, 88; fundamental, 76; to have authority, 29; human, 88,

## ABOUT THE EDITOR

**Richard Bronaugh** is Associate Professor in the Department of Philosophy at the University of Western Ontario, specializing in legal philosophy and the law of contract. His previous book-length work is his co-edited *Agent, Action, and Reason.*

# ABOUT THE AUTHORS

**Joseph Raz** is a Fellow of Balliol College, Oxford. He is the author of *The Concept of a Legal System* (1970) and *Practical Reason and Norms* (1975).

**P. H. Nowell-Smith** is Professor of Philosophy at York University, Toronto. He is the author of *Ethics* (1954).

**Ronald M. Dworkin** is Professor of Jurisprudence at Oxford University. He is the author of *Taking Rights Seriously* (1977) and editor of *The Philosophy of Law* (1977).

**David Lyons** is Professor of Philosophy at Cornell University. He has written *Forms and Limits of Utilitarianism* (1965) and *In the Interest of the Governed* (1973).

**Mark R. MacGuigan** has been Member of Parliament for Windsor-Walkerville, Ontario, Canada, since 1968 and was formerly Dean of Law at the University of Windsor. He is the author of *Jurisprudence: Readings and Cases* (1966).

**Martin P. Golding** is Professor of Philosophy at Duke University. He is the author of *Philosophy of Law* (1975) and editor of *The Nature of Law* (1966).

**Robert S. Summers** is Professor of Law at Cornell University. He is the coauthor (with Charles G. Howard) of *Law: Its Nature, Functions, and Limits* (1965) and the editor of *Essays in Legal Philosophy* (1968) and *More Essays on Legal Philosophy* (1971).

**Morley R. Gorsky** is Professor of Law at the University of Western Ontario. He is the coauthor (with Innis Christie) of *Unfair Labour Practices* (1969).

**David Flaherty** is Professor of History at the University of Western Ontario and the author of *Privacy in Colonial New England* (1972).

**Richard A. Wasserstrom** is Professor of Law and Professor of Philosophy at UCLA. He is the author of *The Judicial Decision* (1961) and the editor of *Morality and the Law* (1971), *War and Morality* (1970), and *Today's Moral Problems* (1975).

**Lorenne M. G. Clark** is Associate Professor, Department of Philosophy and Centre of Criminology, at the University of Toronto.

**Howard Cohen** is Associate Professor of Philosophy at the University of Massachusetts, Boston.